STAR WARS®

CLONE WARS
ADVENTURES
VOLUME 6

designer
Joshua Elliott

assistant editor
Dave Marshall

editor
Jeremy Barlow

publisher
Mike Richardson

special thanks to Sue Rostoni, Leland Chee,
and Amy Gary at Lucas Licensing

The events in this story take place
just before and during the events in
Star Wars: Episode III *Revenge of the Sith*

www.titanbooks.com
www.starwars.com

STAR WARS: CLONE WARS ADVENTURES Volume 6, October 2006. Published
by Titan Books, a division of Titan Publishing Group Ltd., 144 Southwark Street,
London SE1 0UP. Star Wars ©2006 Lucasfilm Ltd. & ™. All rights reserved. Used
under authorization. Text and illustrations for Star Wars are © 2006 Lucasfilm Ltd. No
portion of this publication may be reproduced or transmitted, in any form or by any
means, without the express written permission of the copyright holder, Inc. Names,
characters, places, and incidents featured in this publication either are the product of
the author's imagination or are used fictitiously. Any resemblance to actual persons
(living or dead), events, institutions, or locales, without satiric intent, is coincidental.
PRINTED IN ITALY

2 4 6 8 10 9 7 5 3 1

STAR WARS®
CLONE WARS
ADVENTURES
VOLUME 6

"IT TAKES A THIEF"
script and art **The Fillbach Brothers**
colors **Ronda Pattison**

"THE DROP"
script **Mike Kennedy**
art **Stewart McKenney**
colors **Ronda Pattison**

"TO THE VANISHING POINT"
script and art **The Fillbach Brothers**
colors **Ronda Pattison**

"MEANS AND ENDS"
script **Haden Blackman**
art **Rick Lacy**
colors **Dan Jackson**

lettering
Michael David Thomas

cover
The Fillbach Brothers and Dan Jackson

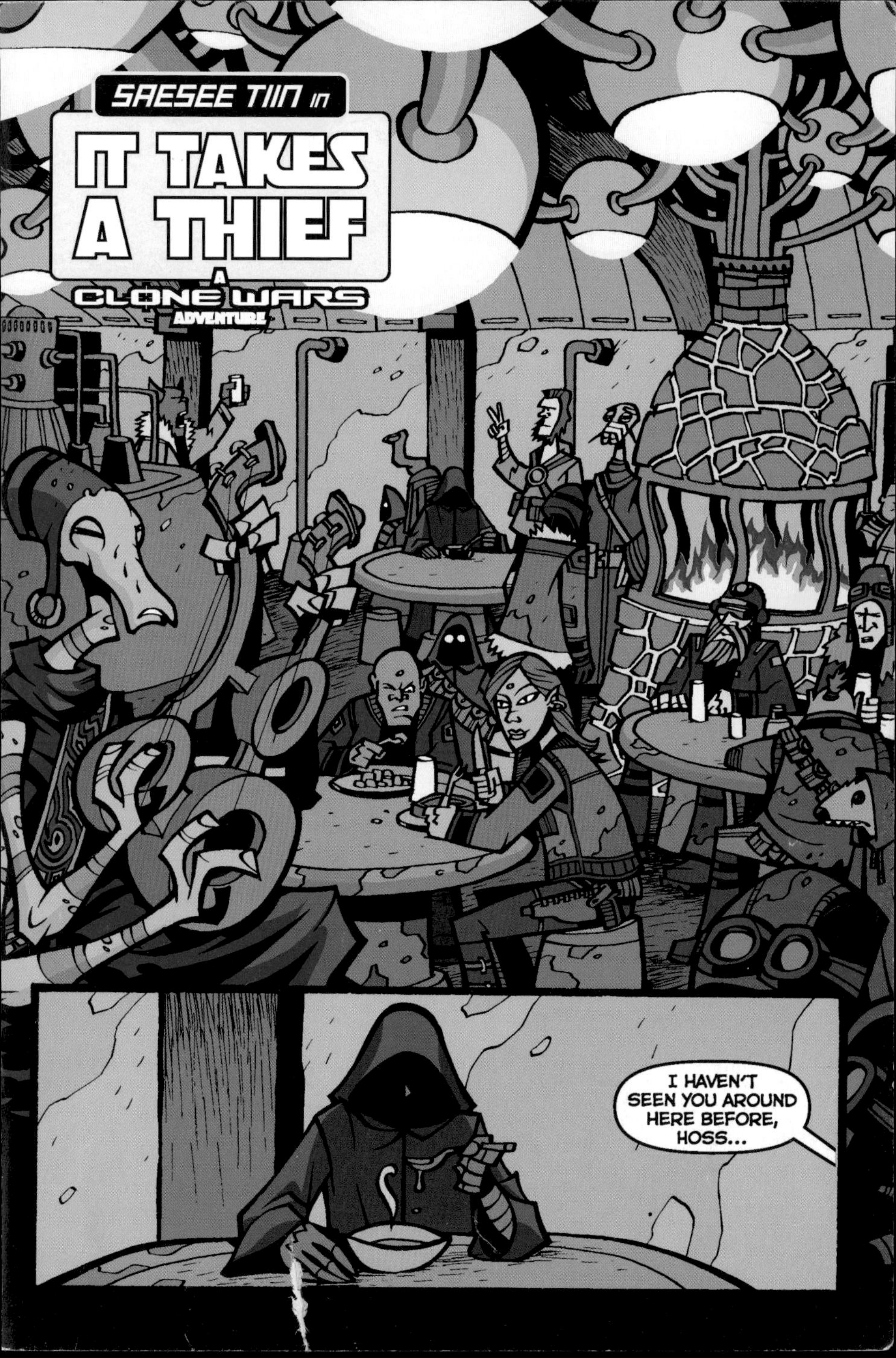
SAESEE TIIN in
IT TAKES A THIEF
A CLONE WARS ADVENTURE
I HAVEN'T SEEN YOU AROUND HERE BEFORE, HOSS...

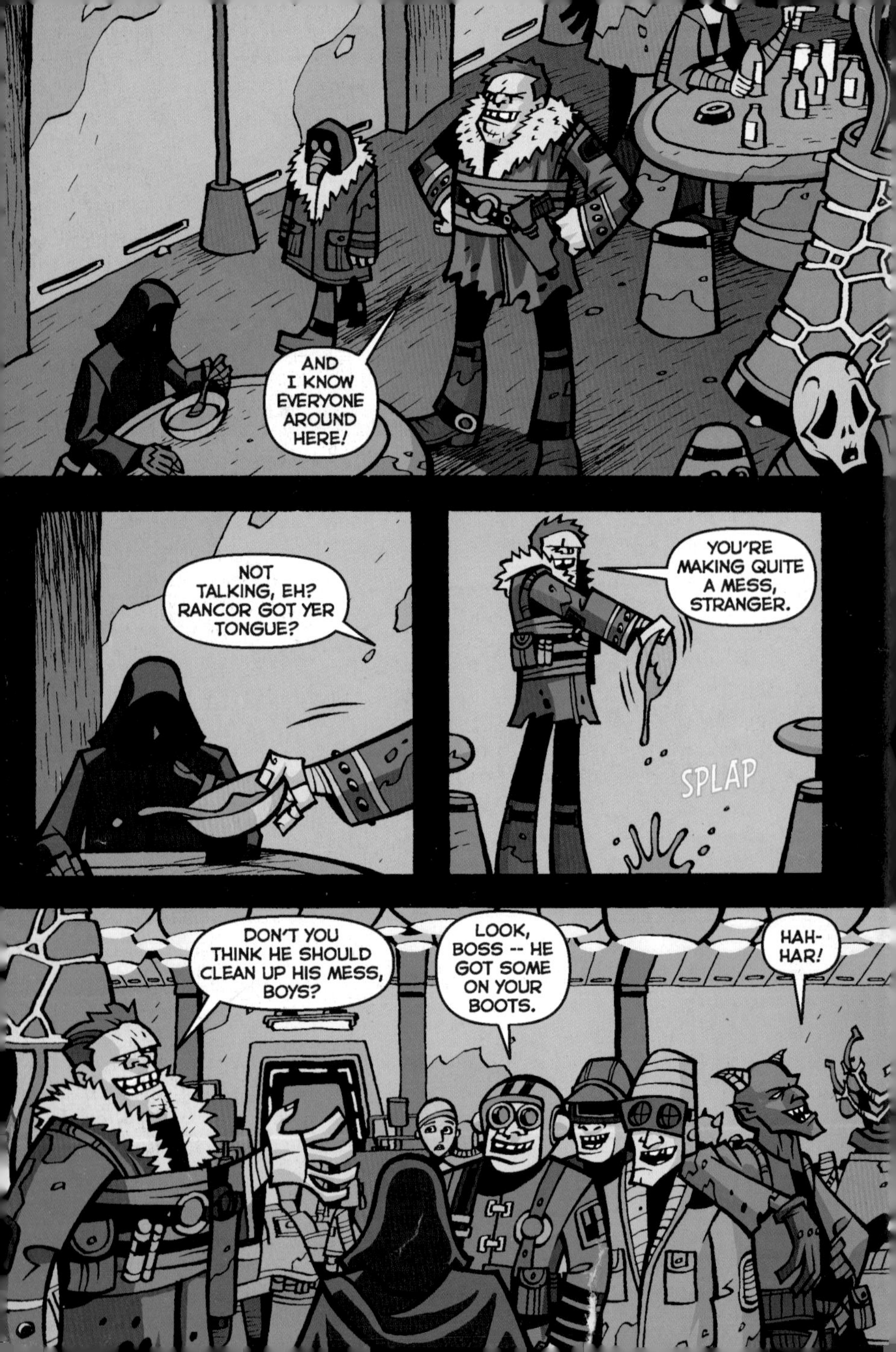
AND I KNOW EVERYONE AROUND HERE!
NOT TALKING, EH? RANCOR GOT YER TONGUE?
YOU'RE MAKING QUITE A MESS, STRANGER.
SPLAP
DON'T YOU THINK HE SHOULD CLEAN UP HIS MESS, BOYS?
LOOK, BOSS -- HE GOT SOME ON YOUR BOOTS.
HAH-HAR!

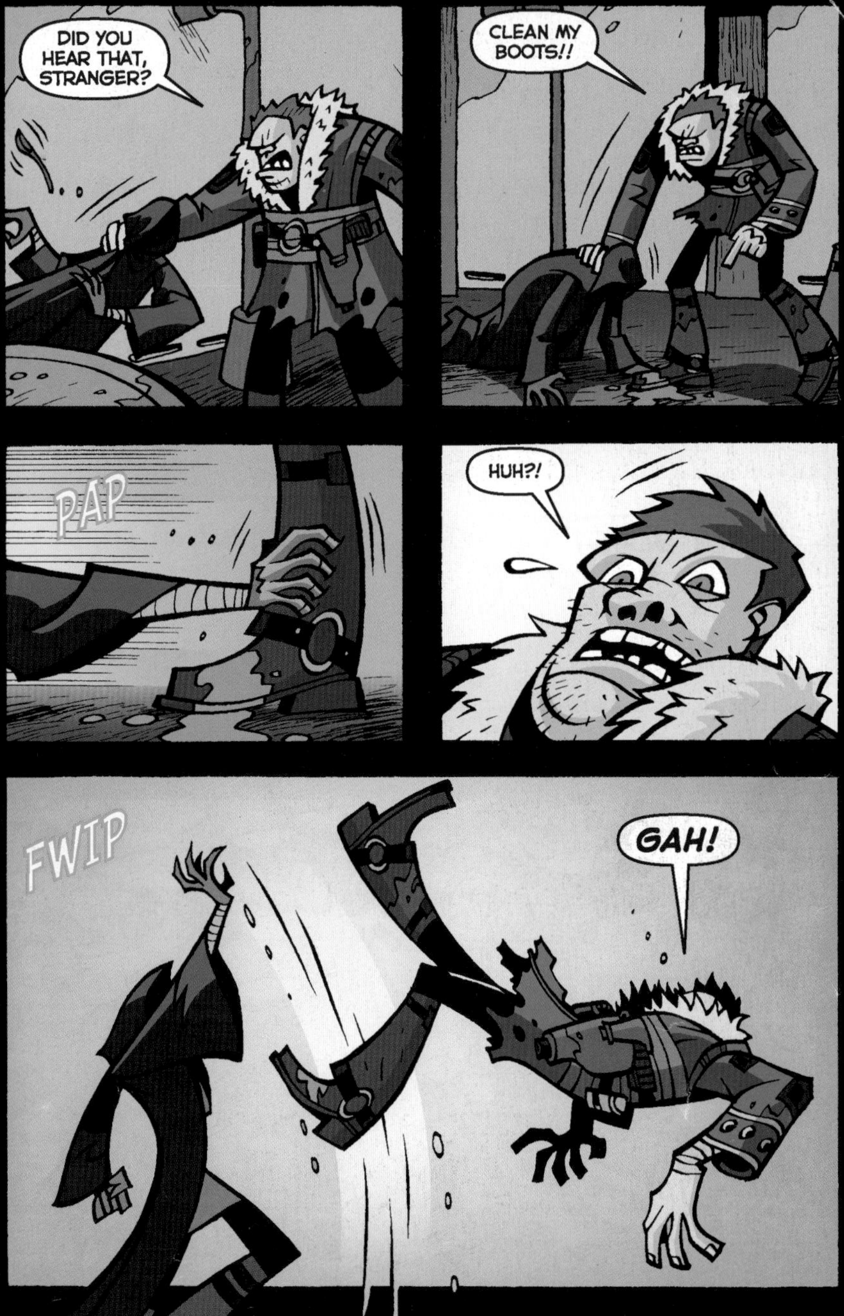
DID YOU HEAR THAT, STRANGER?
CLEAN MY BOOTS!!
PAP
HUH?!
FWIP
GAH!

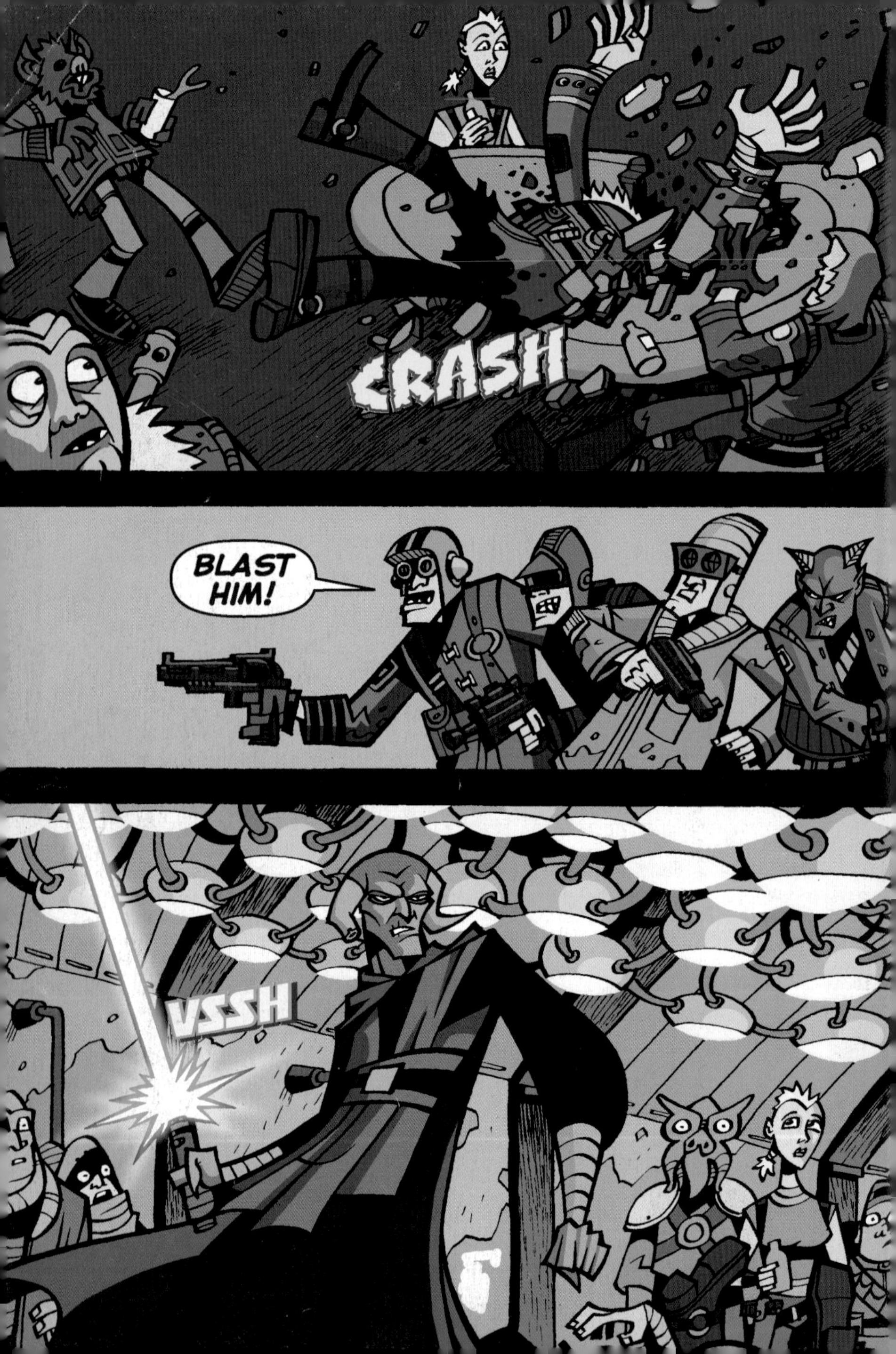
CRASH
BLAST HIM!
VSSH

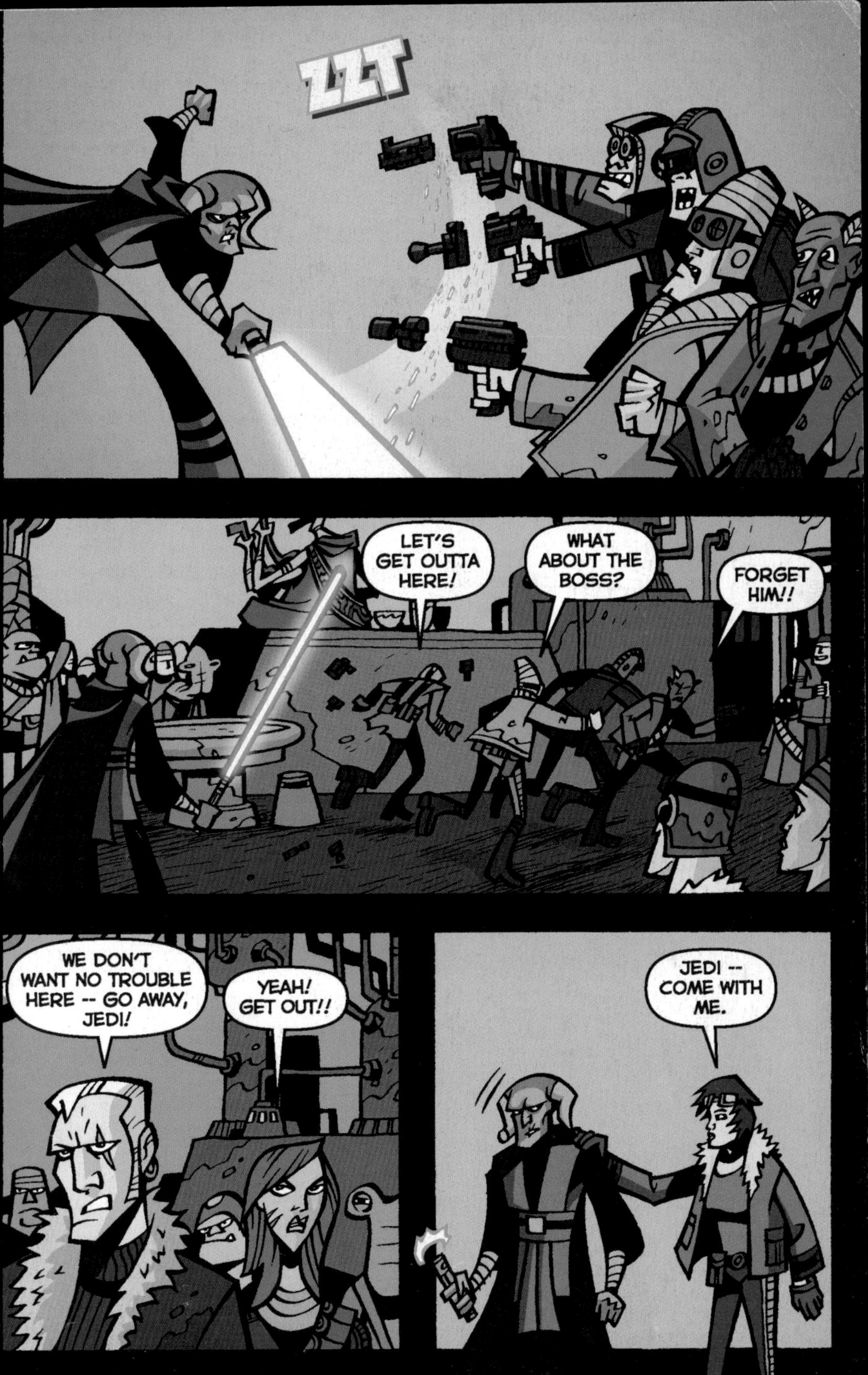
ZZT
LET'S GET OUTTA HERE!
WHAT ABOUT THE BOSS?
FORGET HIM!!
WE DON'T WANT NO TROUBLE HERE -- GO AWAY, JEDI!
YEAH! GET OUT!!
JEDI -- COME WITH ME.

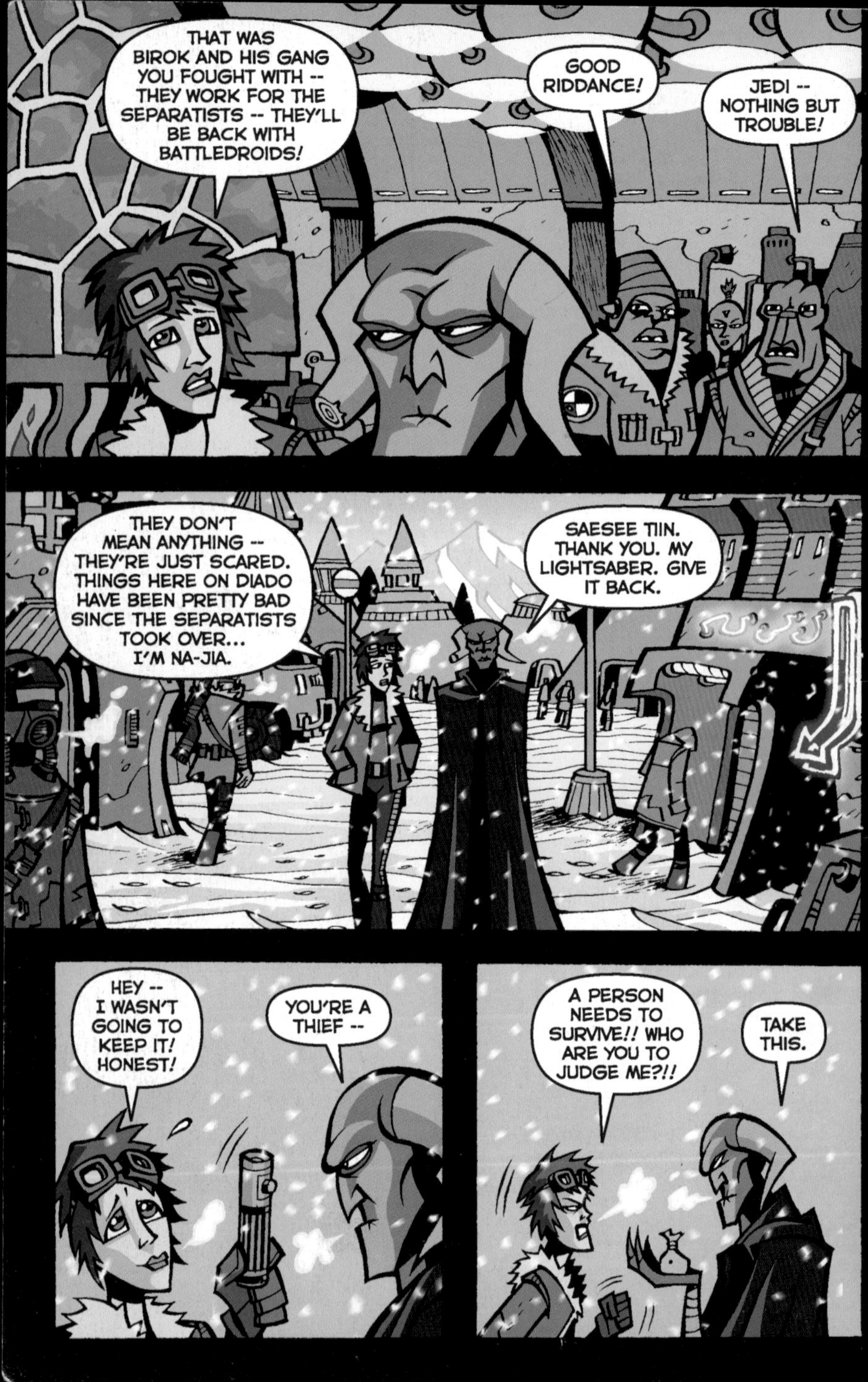
THAT WAS BIROK AND HIS GANG YOU FOUGHT WITH -- THEY WORK FOR THE SEPARATISTS -- THEY'LL BE BACK WITH BATTLEDROIDS!
GOOD RIDDANCE!
JEDI -- NOTHING BUT TROUBLE!
THEY DON'T MEAN ANYTHING -- THEY'RE JUST SCARED. THINGS HERE ON DIADO HAVE BEEN PRETTY BAD SINCE THE SEPARATISTS TOOK OVER... I'M NA-JIA.
SAESEE TIIN. THANK YOU. MY LIGHTSABER. GIVE IT BACK.
HEY -- I WASN'T GOING TO KEEP IT! HONEST!
YOU'RE A THIEF --
A PERSON NEEDS TO SURVIVE!! WHO ARE YOU TO JUDGE ME?!!
TAKE THIS.

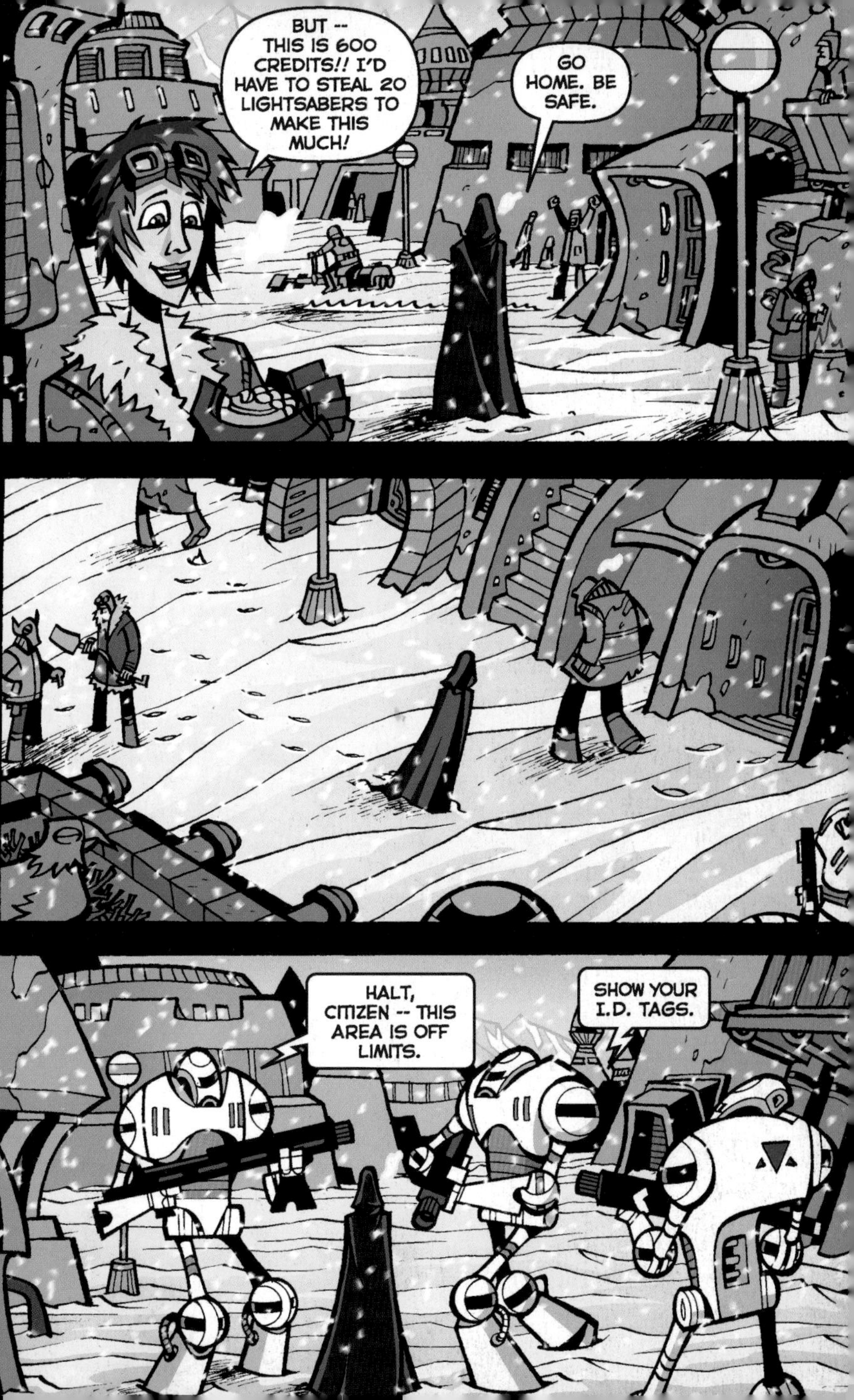
BUT -- THIS IS 600 CREDITS!! I'D HAVE TO STEAL 20 LIGHTSABERS TO MAKE THIS MUCH!
GO HOME. BE SAFE.
HALT, CITIZEN -- THIS AREA IS OFF LIMITS.
SHOW YOUR I.D. TAGS.

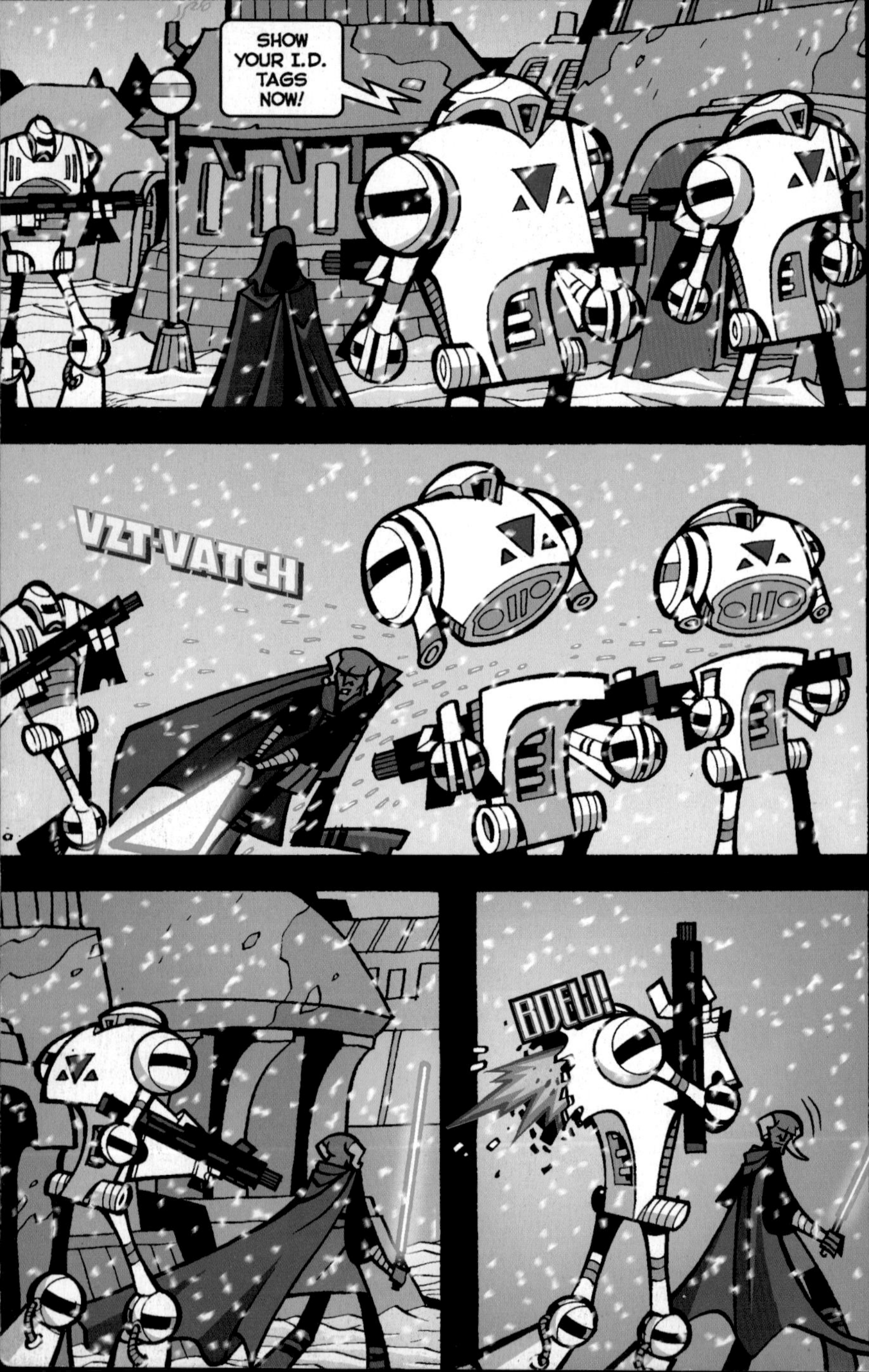
SHOW YOUR I.D. TAGS NOW!
VZT-VATCH
BDEW!

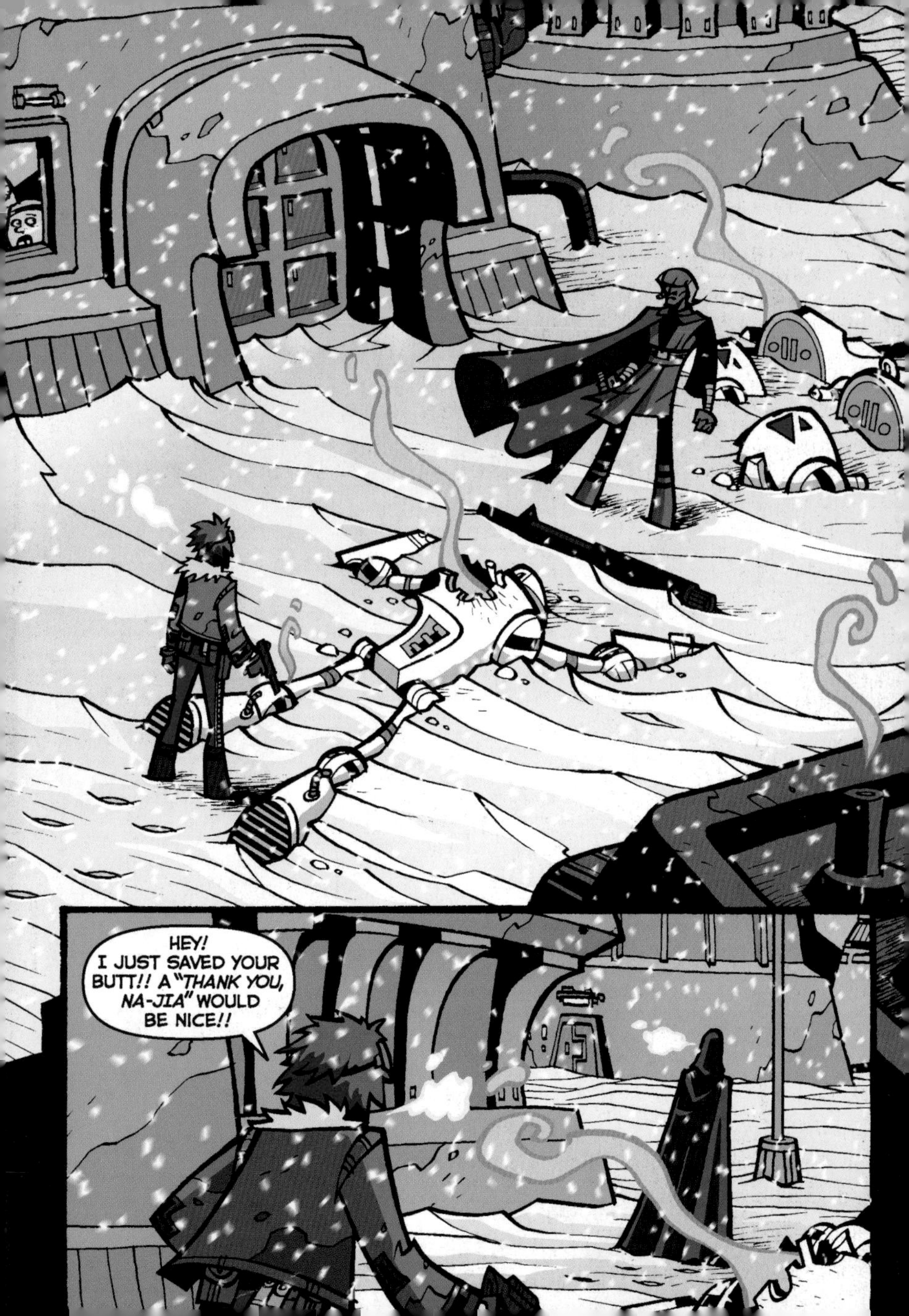
HEY! I JUST SAVED YOUR BUTT!! A "THANK YOU, NA-JIA" WOULD BE NICE!!

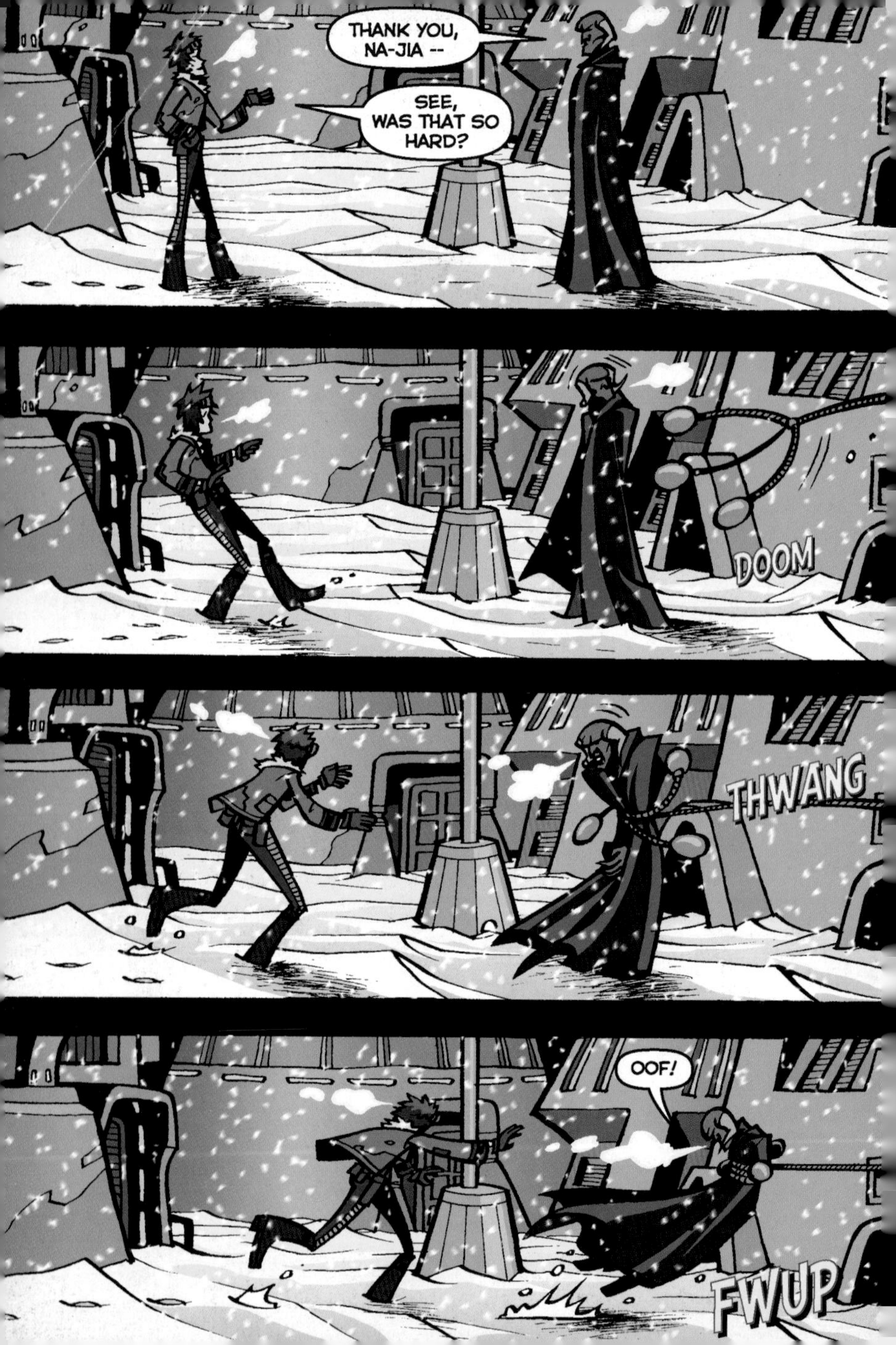
THANK YOU, NA-JIA --
SEE, WAS THAT SO HARD?
DOOM
THWANG
OOF!
FWUP

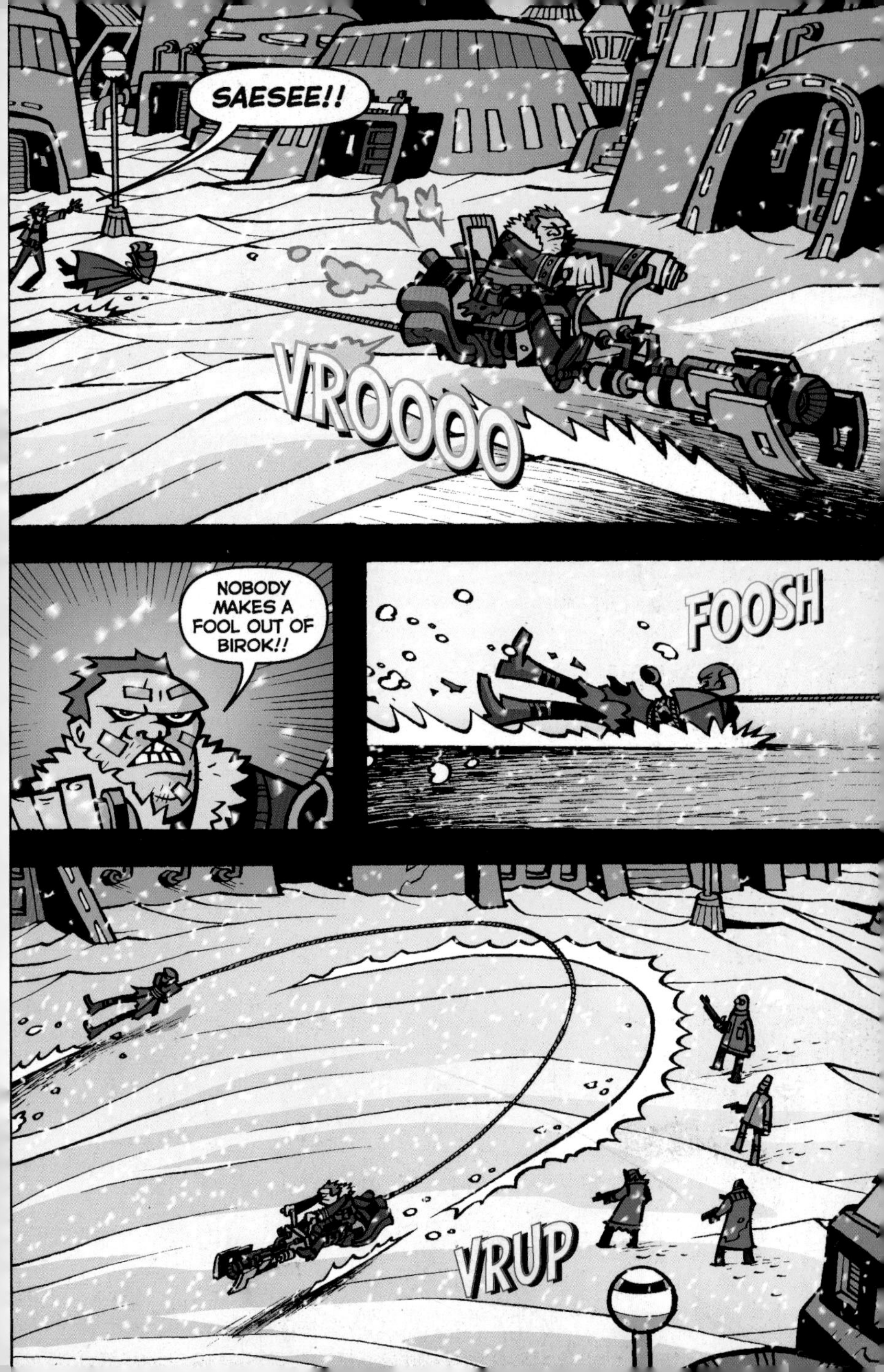
SAESEE!!
VROOOO
NOBODY MAKES A FOOL OUT OF BIROK!!
FOOSH
VRUP

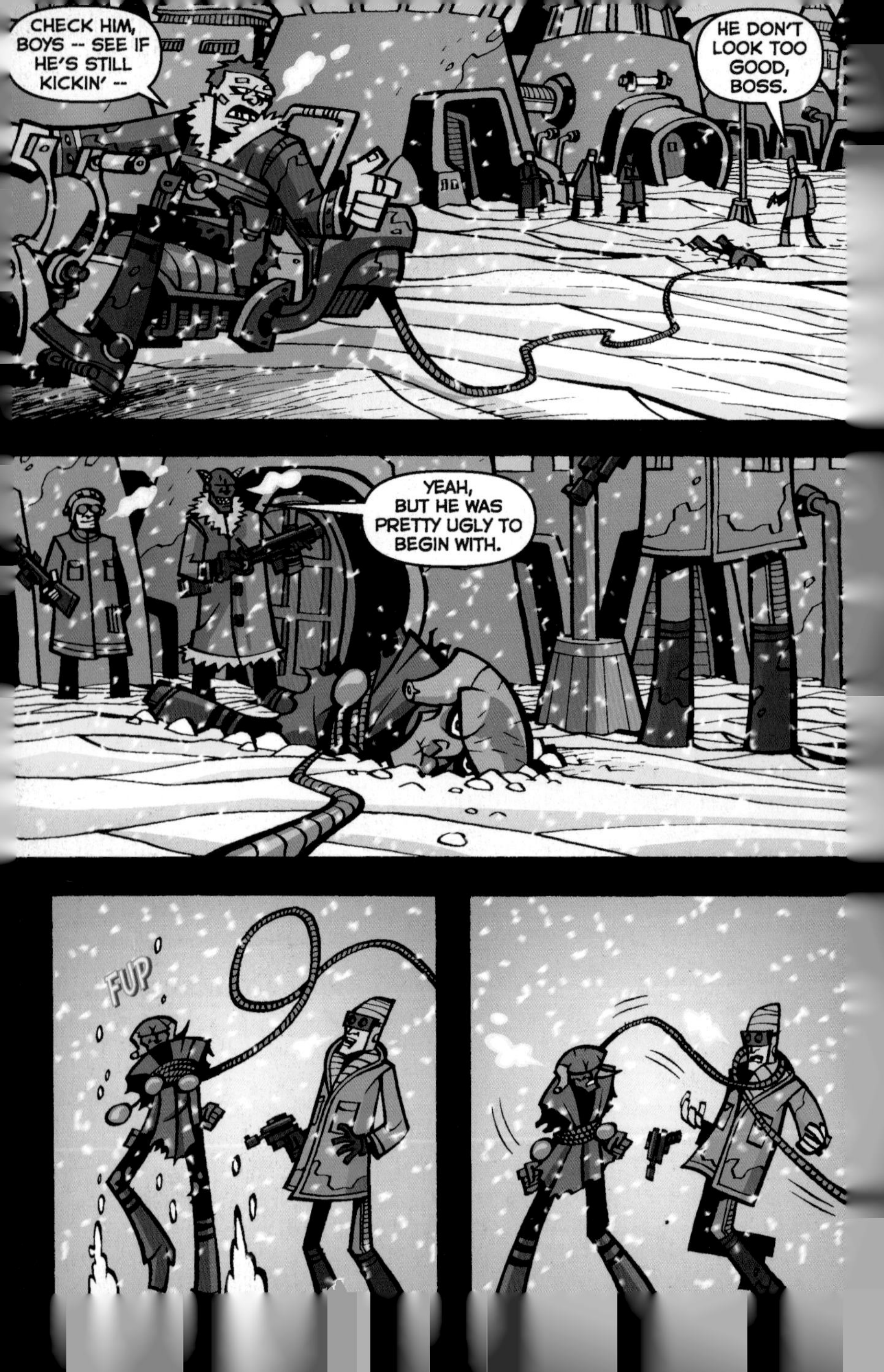
CHECK HIM, BOYS -- SEE IF HE'S STILL KICKIN' --
HE DON'T LOOK TOO GOOD, BOSS.
YEAH, BUT HE WAS PRETTY UGLY TO BEGIN WITH.
FUP

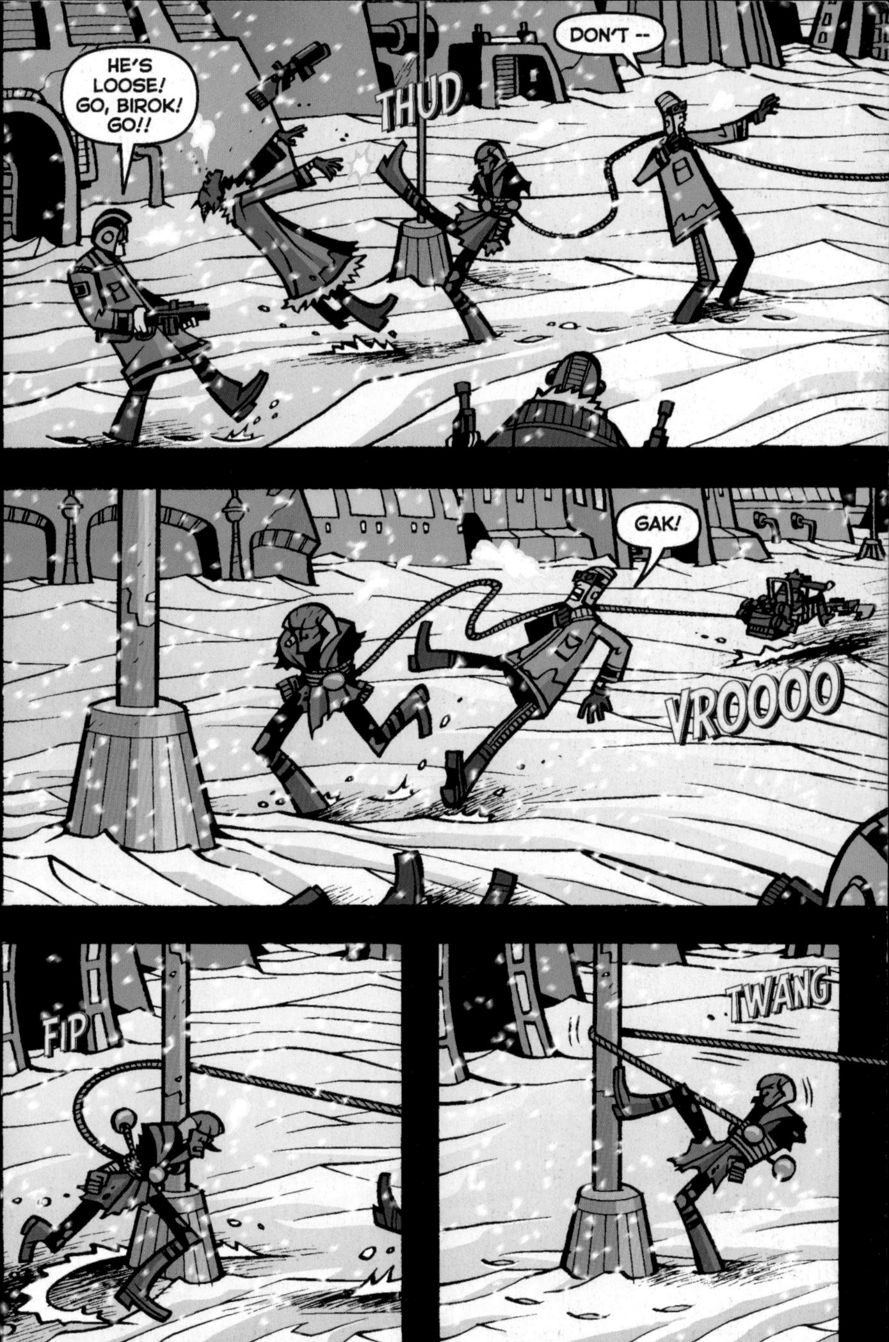
HE'S LOOSE! GO, BIROK! GO!!
THUD
DON'T --
GAK!
VROOOO
FIP
TWANG

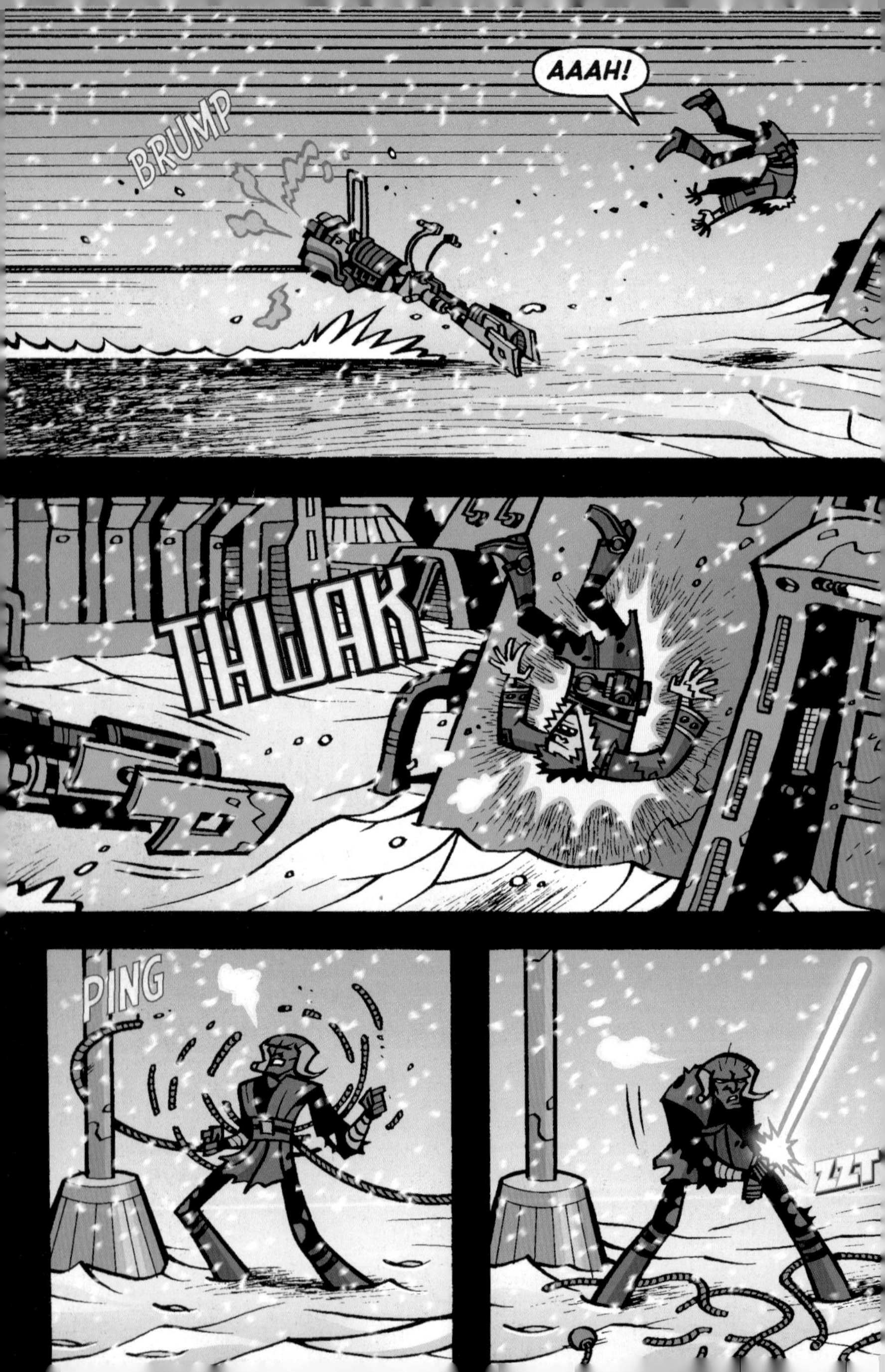
AAAH!
BRUMP
THWAK
PING
ZZT

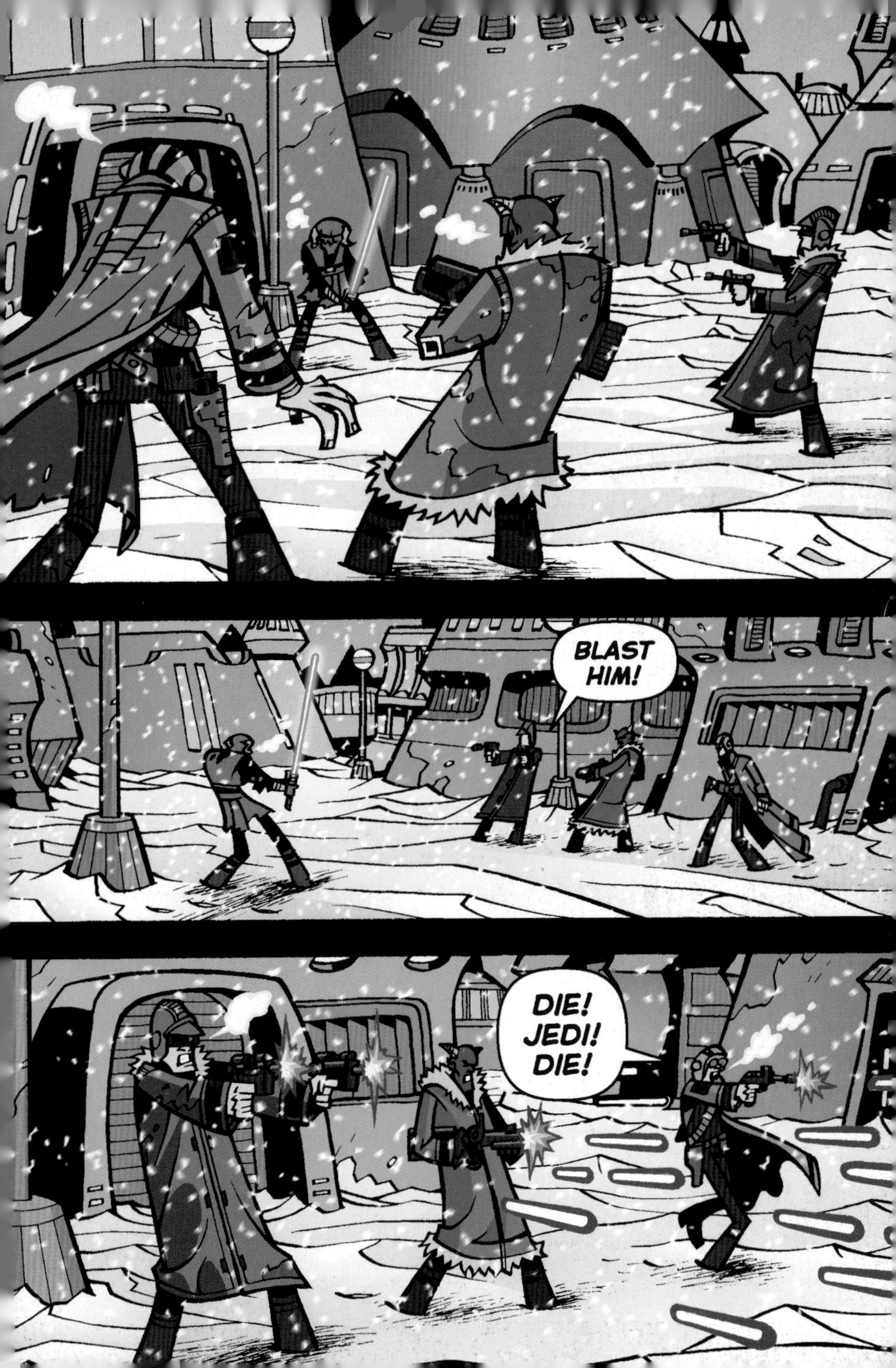
BLAST HIM!
DIE! JEDI! DIE!

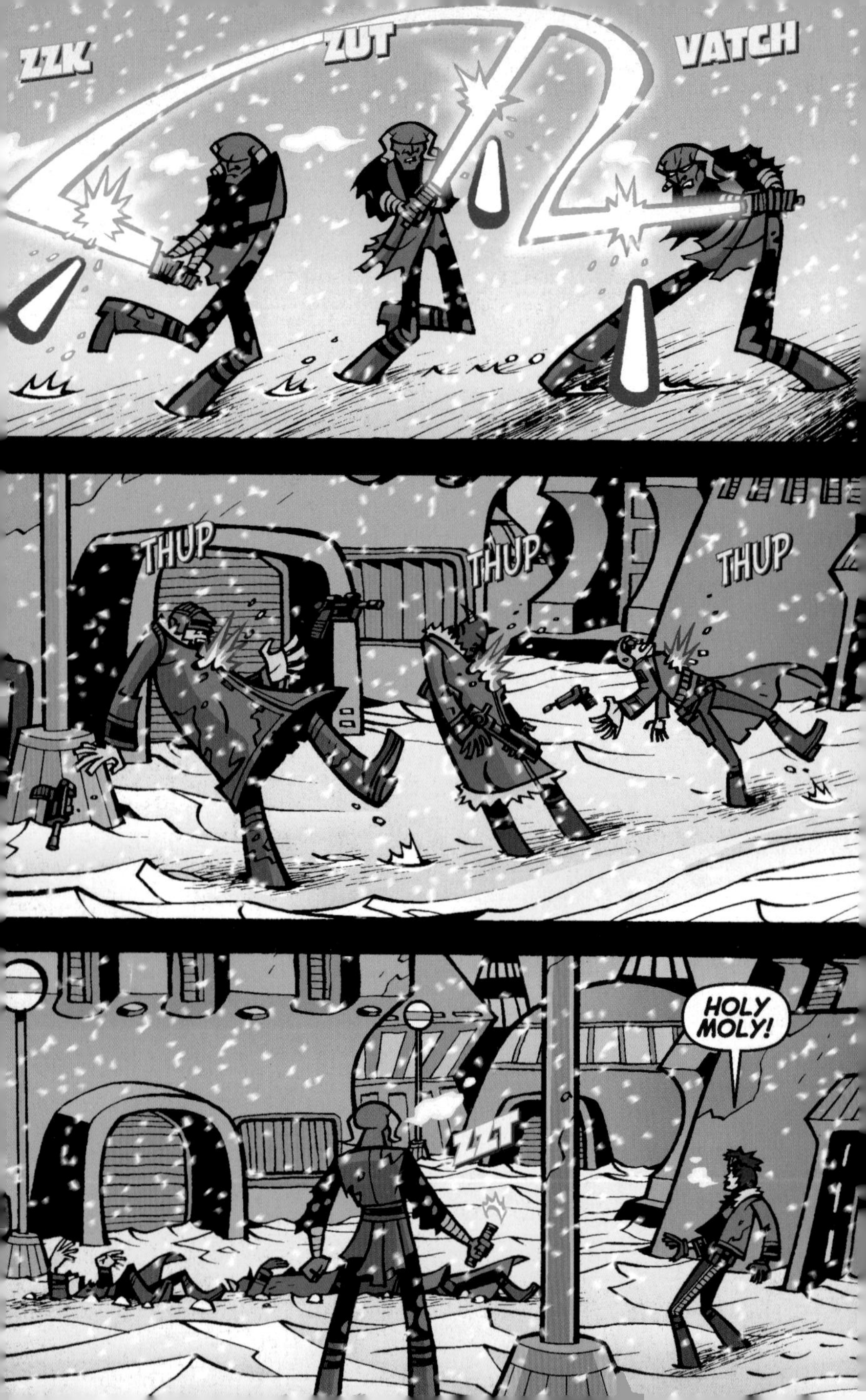
ZZK
ZUT
VATCH
THUP
THUP
THUP
HOLY MOLY!
ZZT

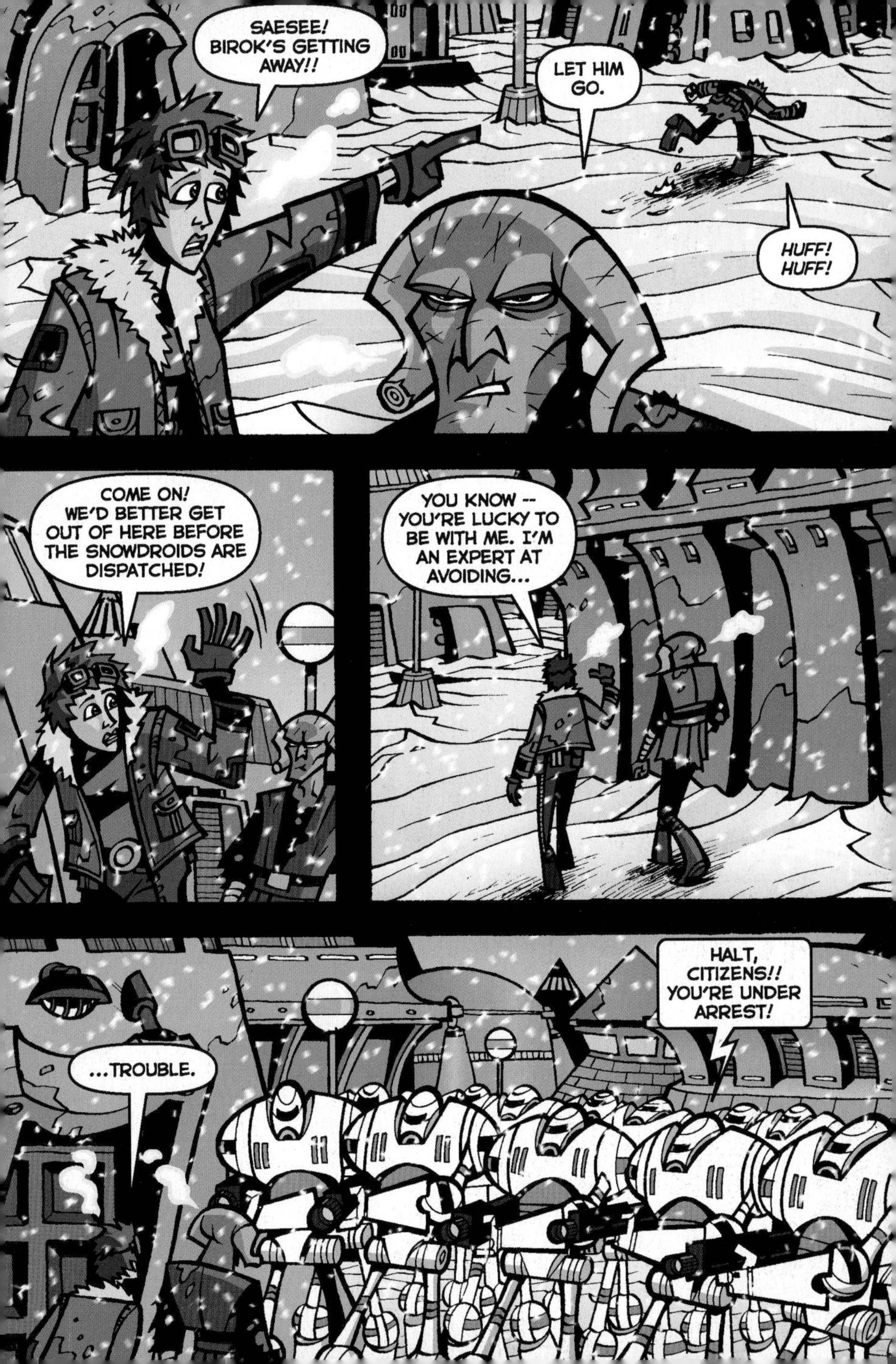
SAESEE! BIROK'S GETTING AWAY!!
LET HIM GO.
HUFF! HUFF!
COME ON! WE'D BETTER GET OUT OF HERE BEFORE THE SNOWDROIDS ARE DISPATCHED!
YOU KNOW -- YOU'RE LUCKY TO BE WITH ME. I'M AN EXPERT AT AVOIDING...
...TROUBLE.
HALT, CITIZENS!! YOU'RE UNDER ARREST!

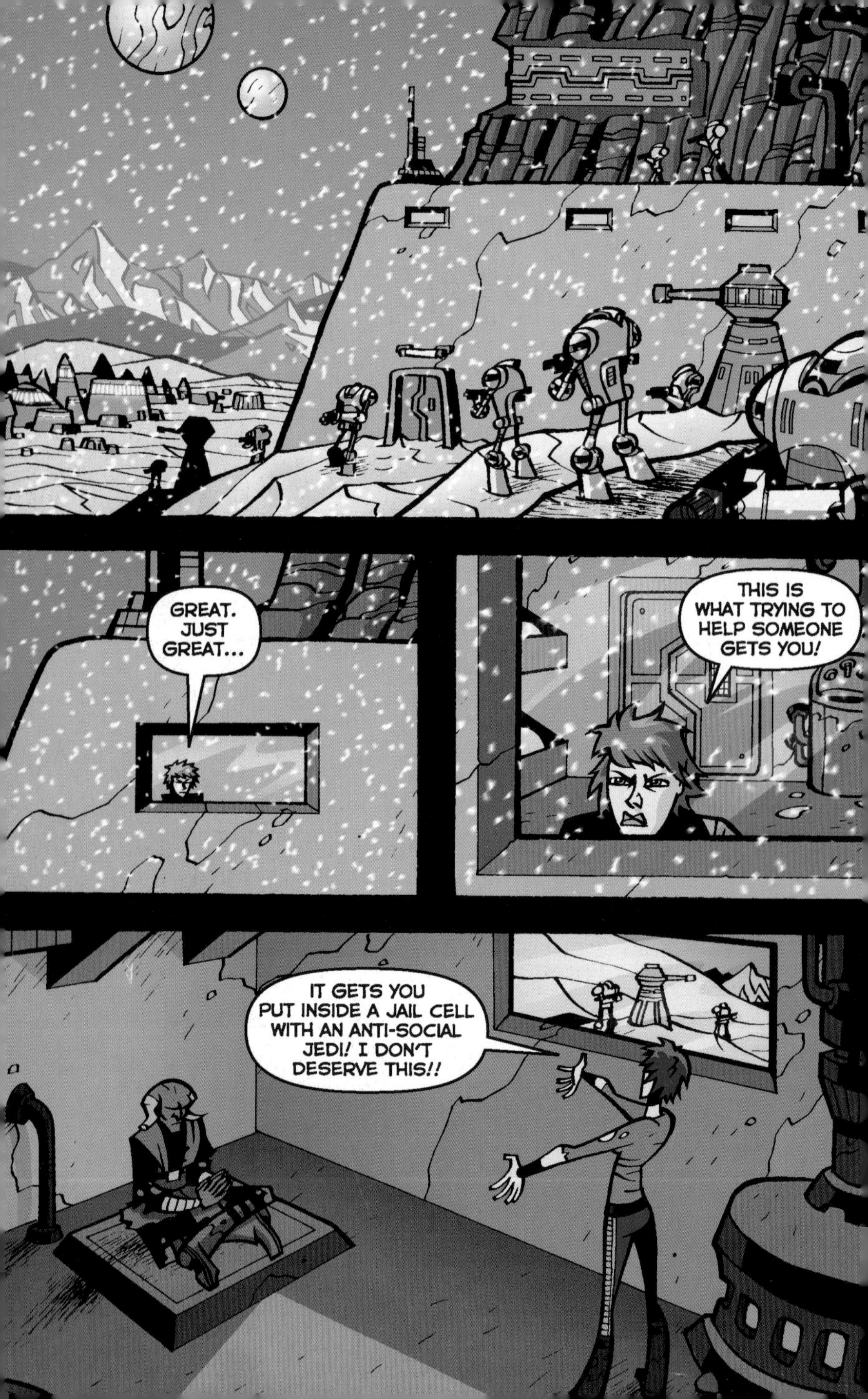
GREAT. JUST GREAT...
THIS IS WHAT TRYING TO HELP SOMEONE GETS YOU!
IT GETS YOU PUT INSIDE A JAIL CELL WITH AN ANTI-SOCIAL JEDI! I DON'T DESERVE THIS!!

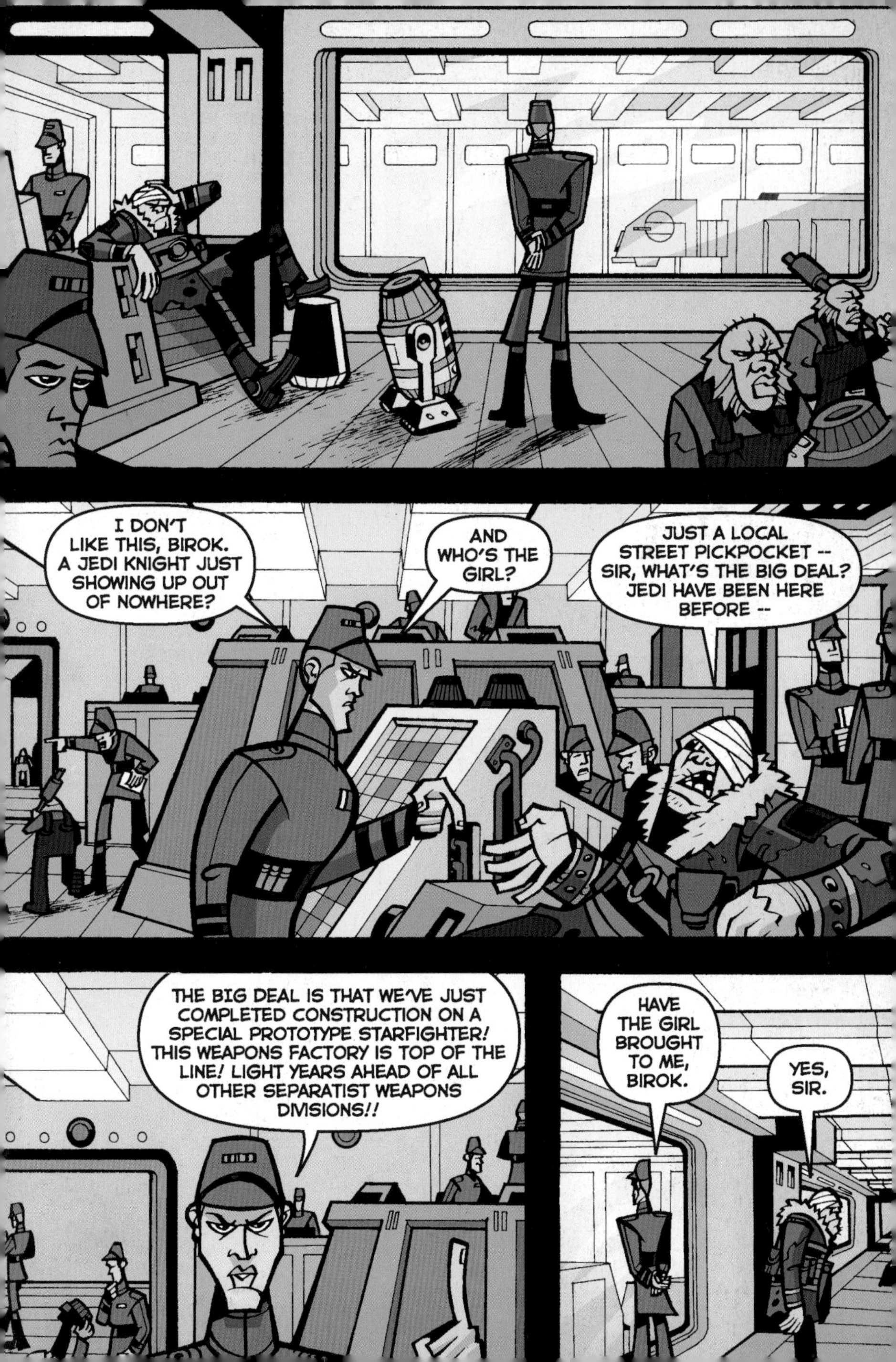
I DON'T LIKE THIS, BIROK. A JEDI KNIGHT JUST SHOWING UP OUT OF NOWHERE?
AND WHO'S THE GIRL?
JUST A LOCAL STREET PICKPOCKET -- SIR, WHAT'S THE BIG DEAL? JEDI HAVE BEEN HERE BEFORE --
THE BIG DEAL IS THAT WE'VE JUST COMPLETED CONSTRUCTION ON A SPECIAL PROTOTYPE STARFIGHTER! THIS WEAPONS FACTORY IS TOP OF THE LINE! LIGHT YEARS AHEAD OF ALL OTHER SEPARATIST WEAPONS DIVISIONS!!
HAVE THE GIRL BROUGHT TO ME, BIROK.
YES, SIR.

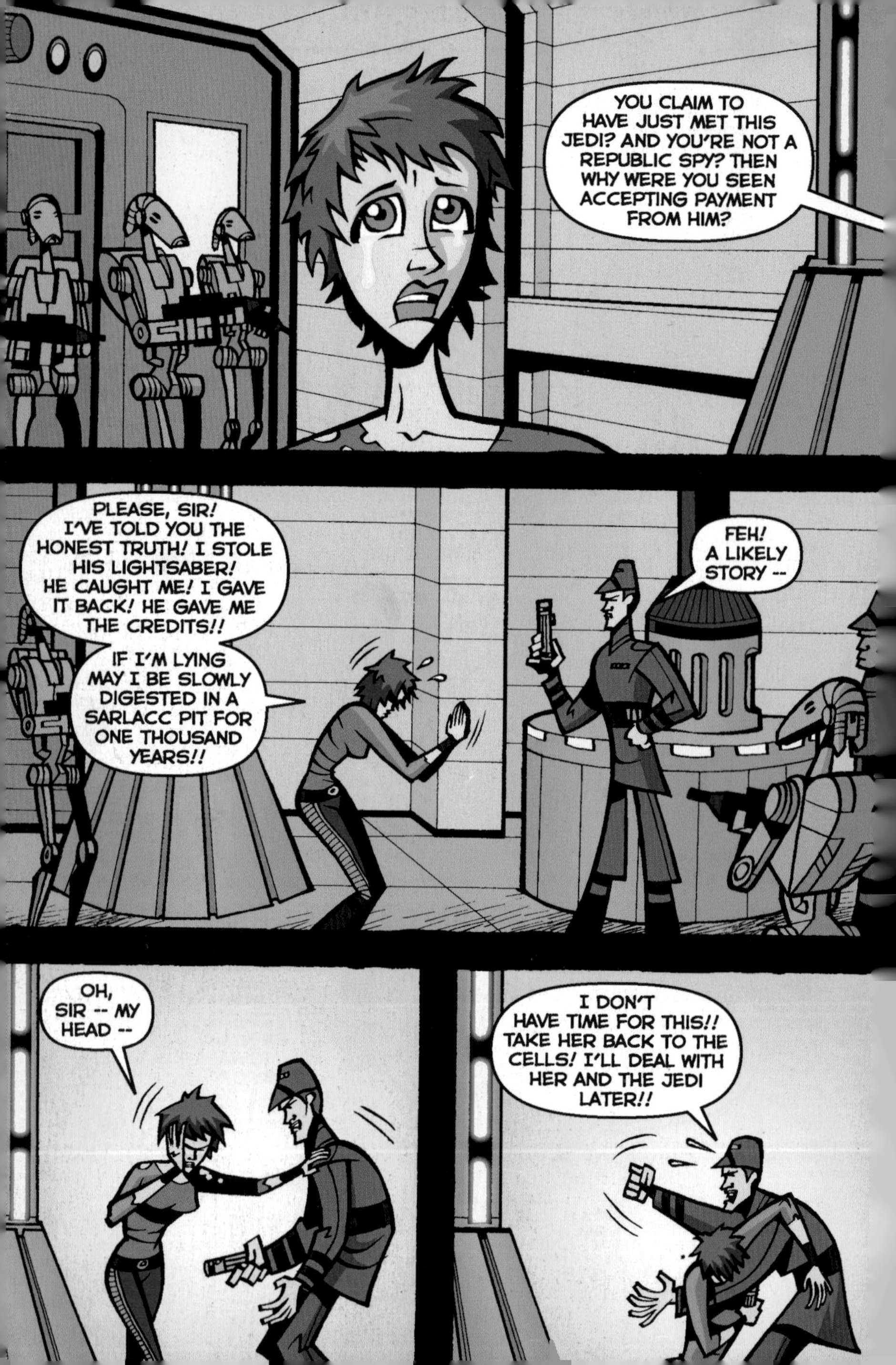
YOU CLAIM TO HAVE JUST MET THIS JEDI? AND YOU'RE NOT A REPUBLIC SPY? THEN WHY WERE YOU SEEN ACCEPTING PAYMENT FROM HIM?
PLEASE, SIR! I'VE TOLD YOU THE HONEST TRUTH! I STOLE HIS LIGHTSABER! HE CAUGHT ME! I GAVE IT BACK! HE GAVE ME THE CREDITS!!
IF I'M LYING MAY I BE SLOWLY DIGESTED IN A SARLACC PIT FOR ONE THOUSAND YEARS!!
FEH! A LIKELY STORY --
OH, SIR -- MY HEAD --
I DON'T HAVE TIME FOR THIS!! TAKE HER BACK TO THE CELLS! I'LL DEAL WITH HER AND THE JEDI LATER!!

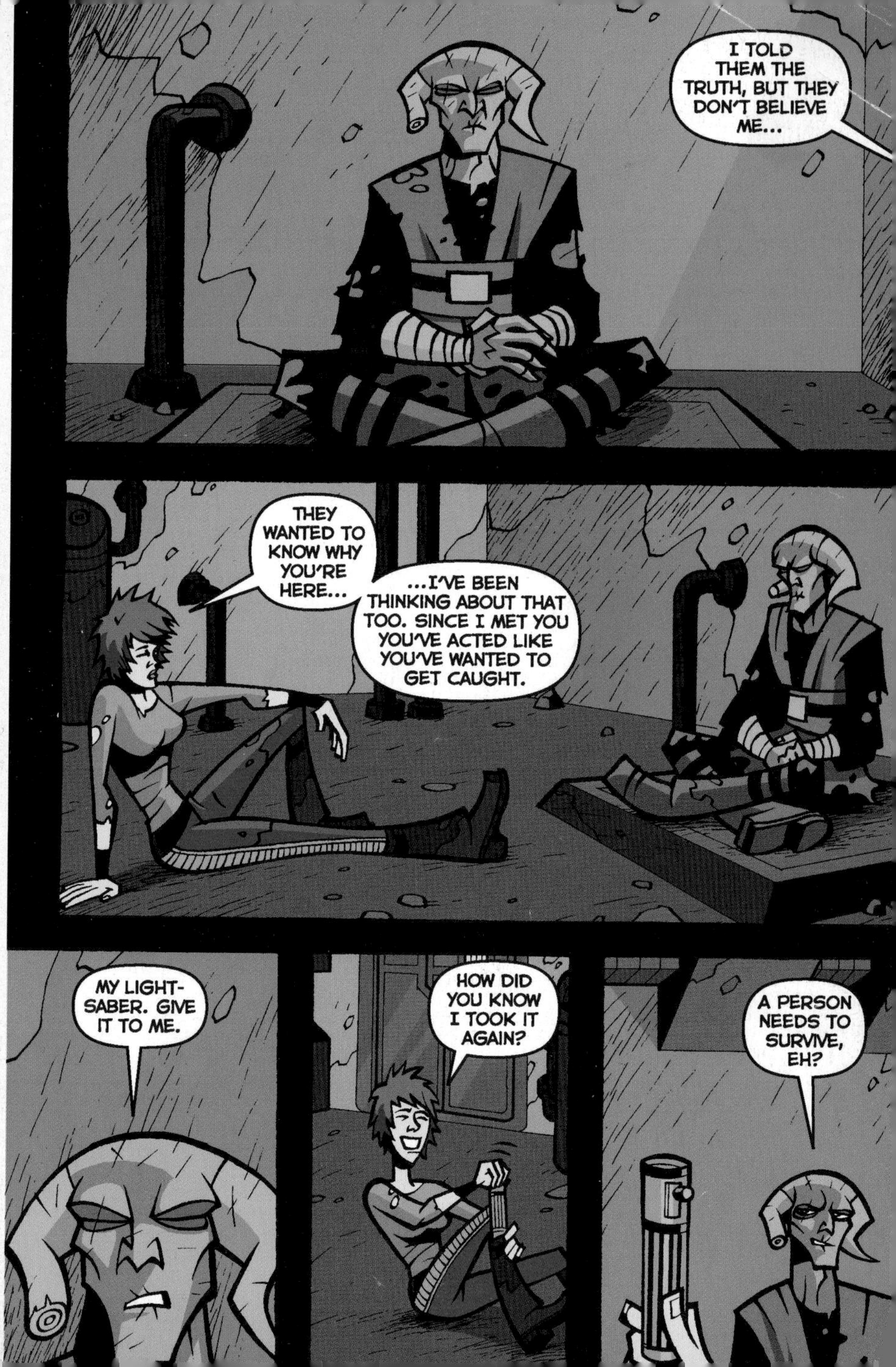

I TOLD THEM THE TRUTH, BUT THEY DON'T BELIEVE ME...
THEY WANTED TO KNOW WHY YOU'RE HERE...
...I'VE BEEN THINKING ABOUT THAT TOO. SINCE I MET YOU YOU'VE ACTED LIKE YOU'VE WANTED TO GET CAUGHT.
MY LIGHT-SABER. GIVE IT TO ME.
HOW DID YOU KNOW I TOOK IT AGAIN?
A PERSON NEEDS TO SURVIVE, EH?

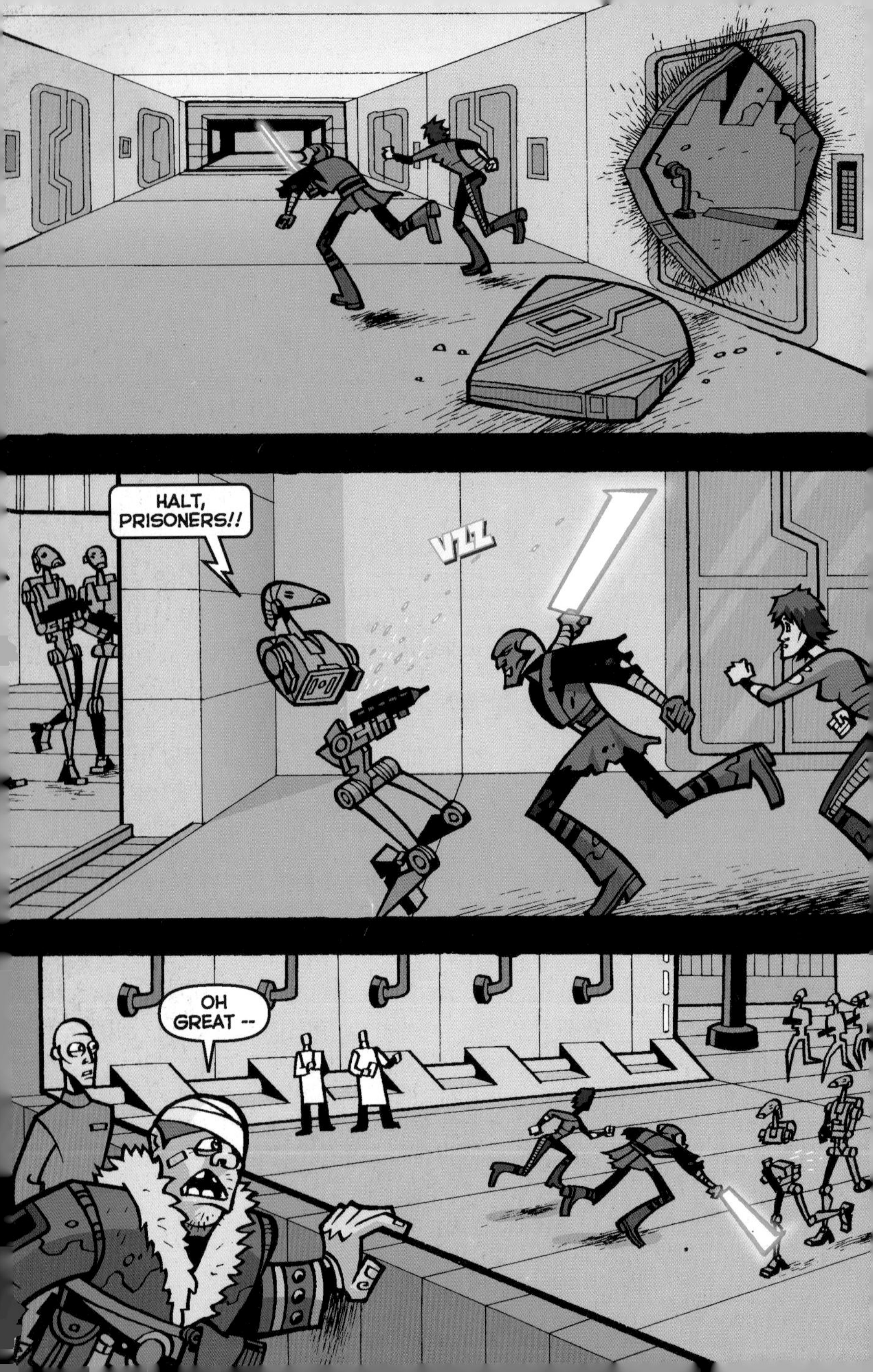
HALT, PRISONERS!!
VZZ
OH GREAT --

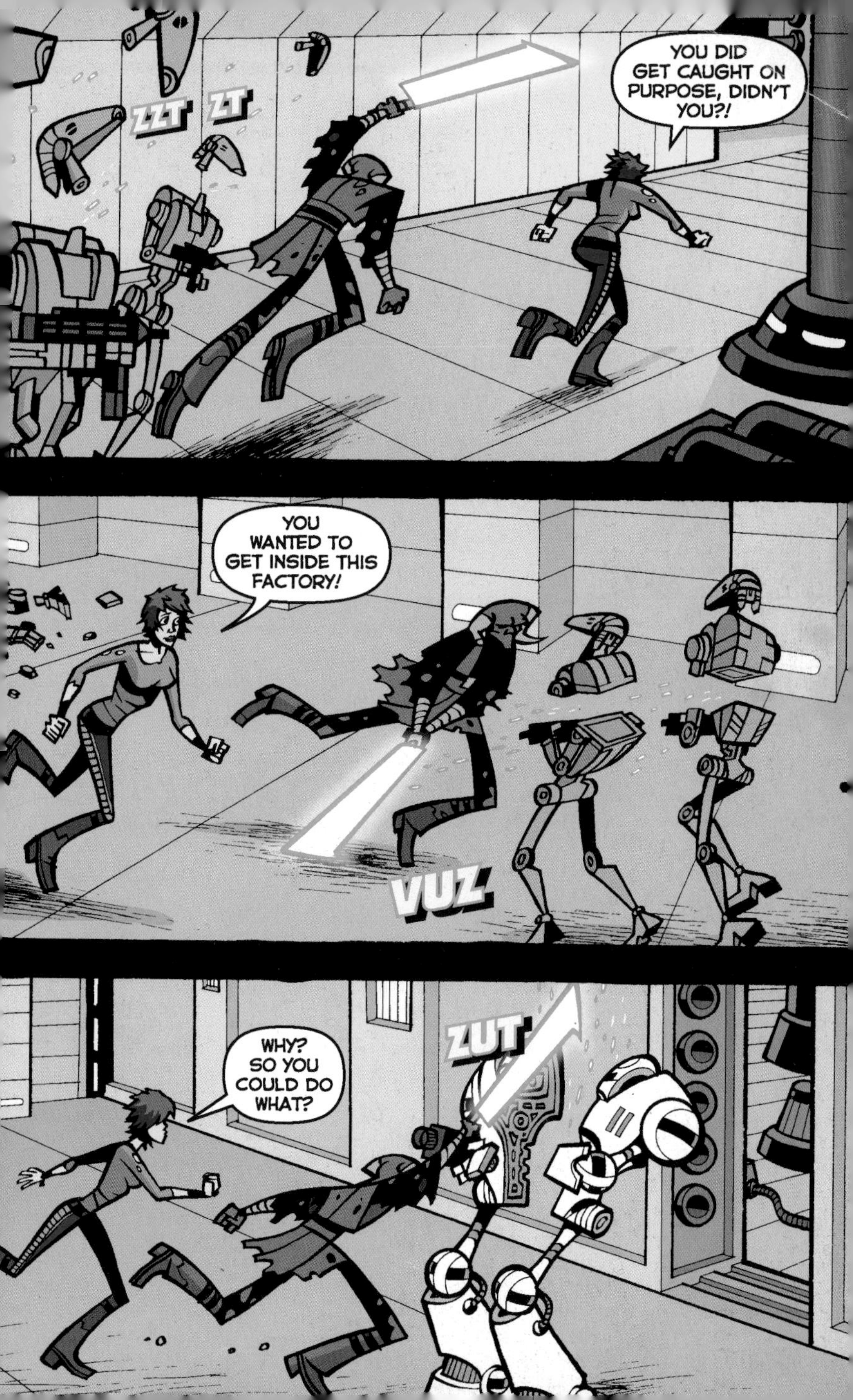
ZZT ZT
YOU DID GET CAUGHT ON PURPOSE, DIDN'T YOU?!
YOU WANTED TO GET INSIDE THIS FACTORY!
VUZ
WHY? SO YOU COULD DO WHAT?
ZUT

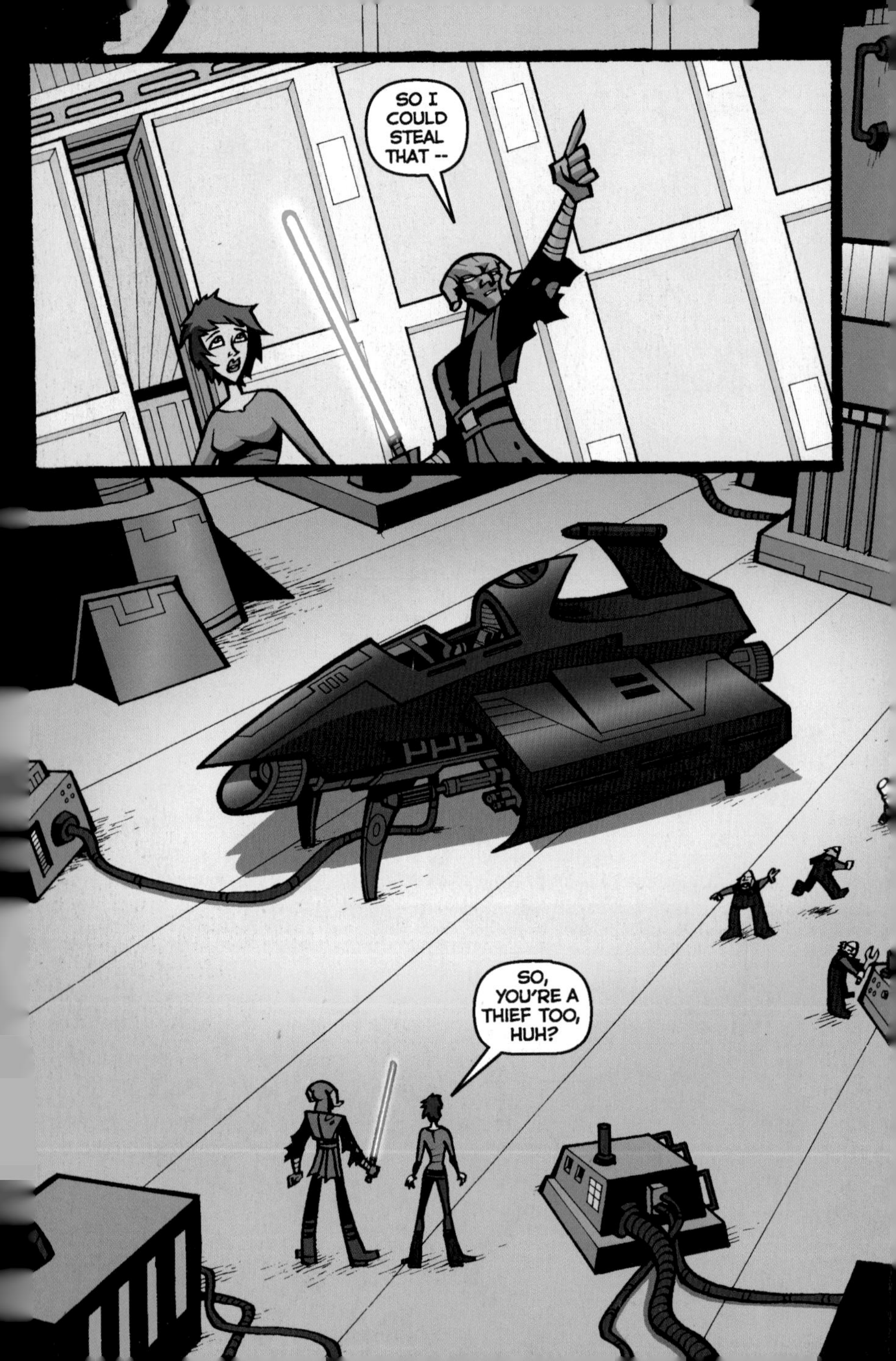
SO I COULD STEAL THAT --
SO, YOU'RE A THIEF TOO, HUH?

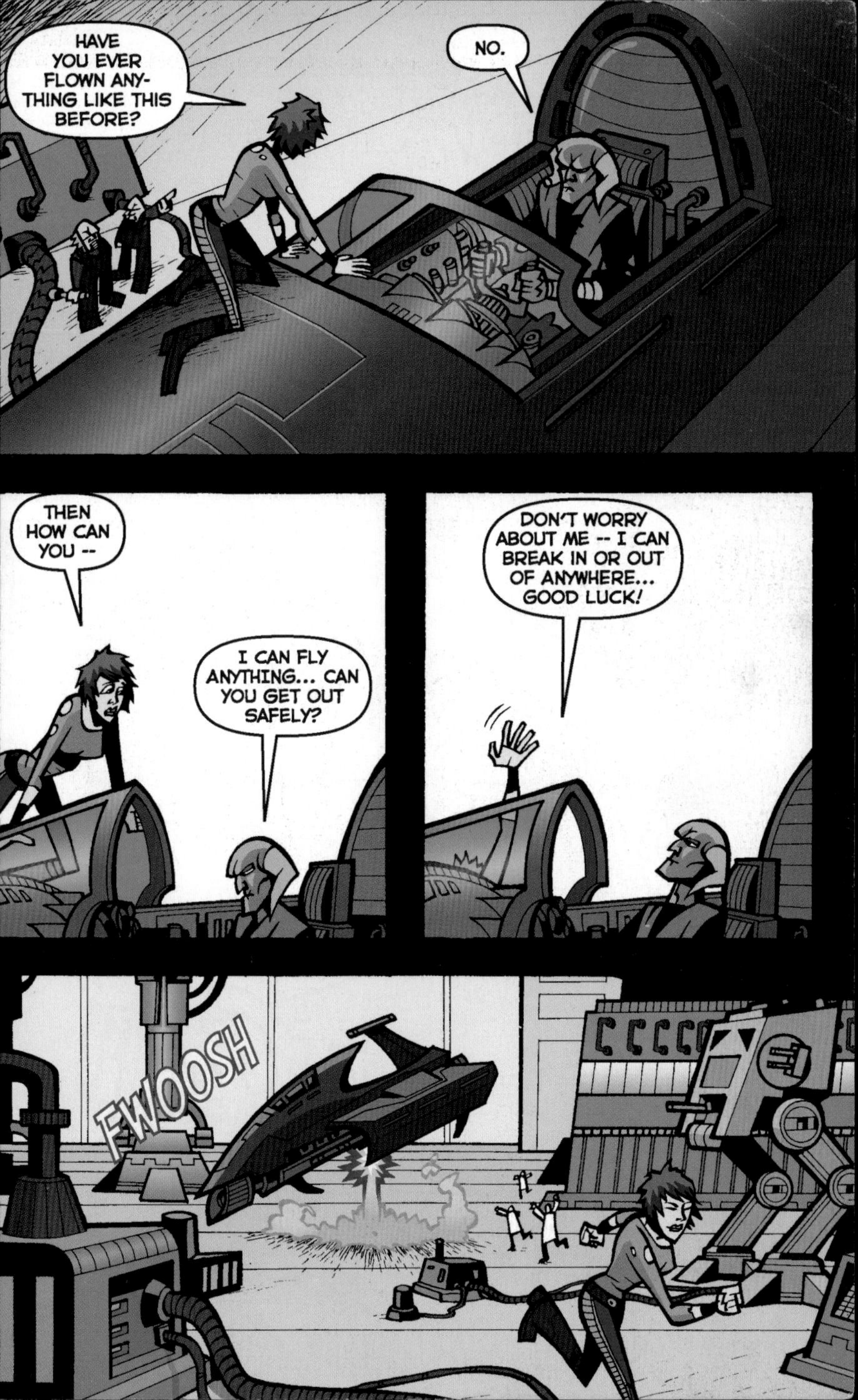
HAVE YOU EVER FLOWN ANY-THING LIKE THIS BEFORE?
NO.
THEN HOW CAN YOU --
I CAN FLY ANYTHING... CAN YOU GET OUT SAFELY?
DON'T WORRY ABOUT ME -- I CAN BREAK IN OR OUT OF ANYWHERE... GOOD LUCK!
FWOOSH

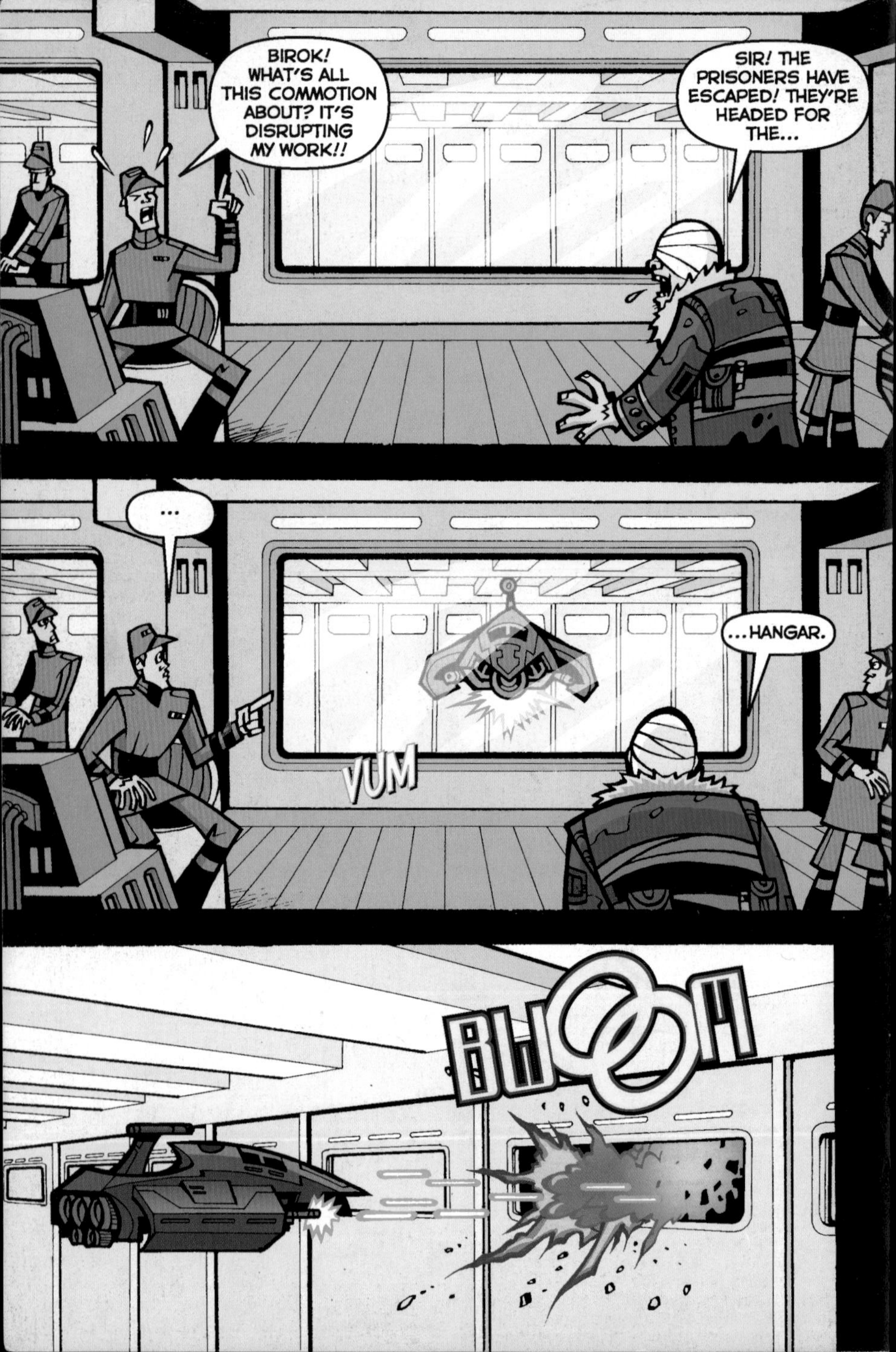
BIROK! WHAT'S ALL THIS COMMOTION ABOUT? IT'S DISRUPTING MY WORK!!
SIR! THE PRISONERS HAVE ESCAPED! THEY'RE HEADED FOR THE...
...
...HANGAR.
VUM
BLOOM

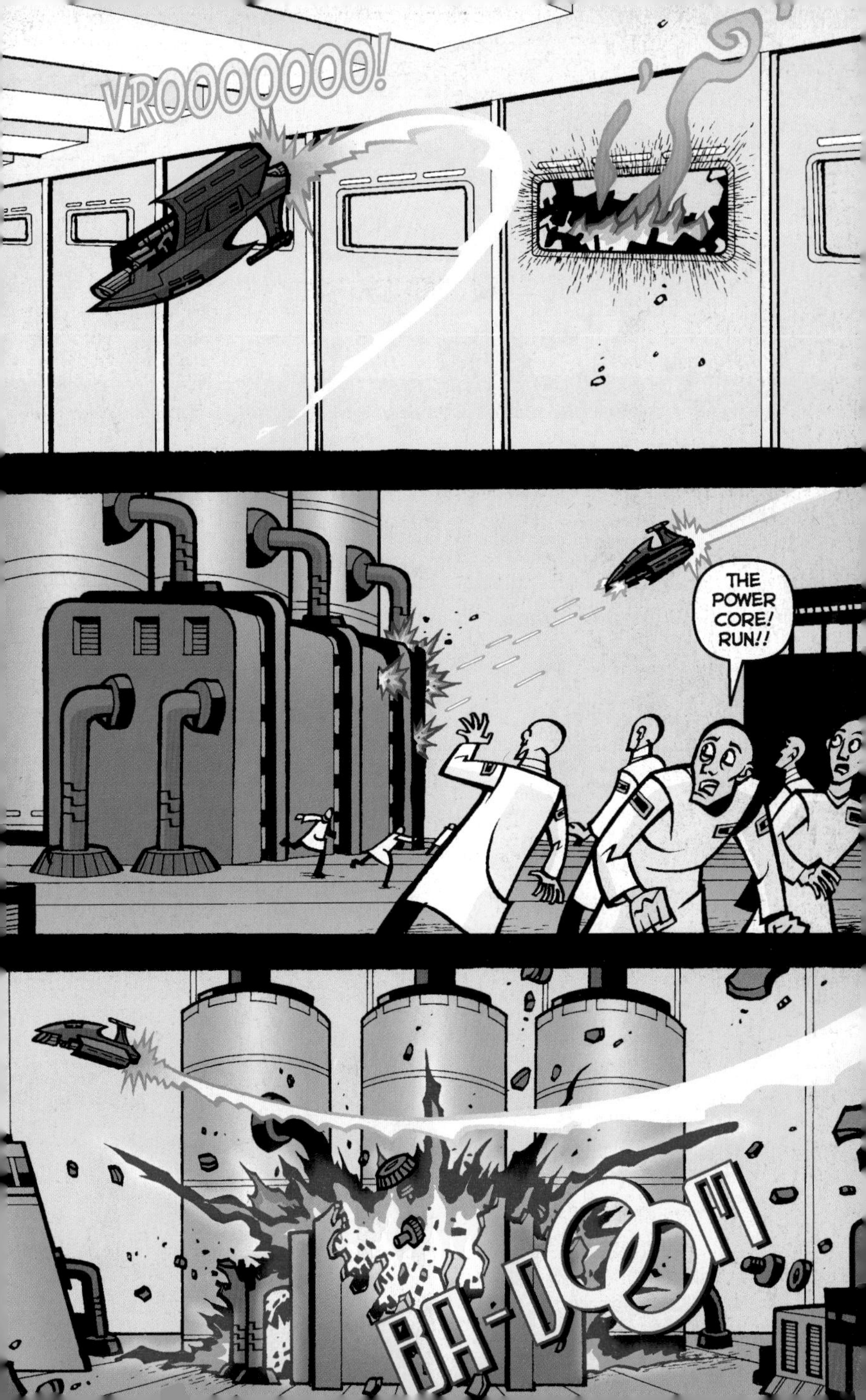
VROOOOOOO!
THE POWER CORE! RUN!!
BA-DOOM!

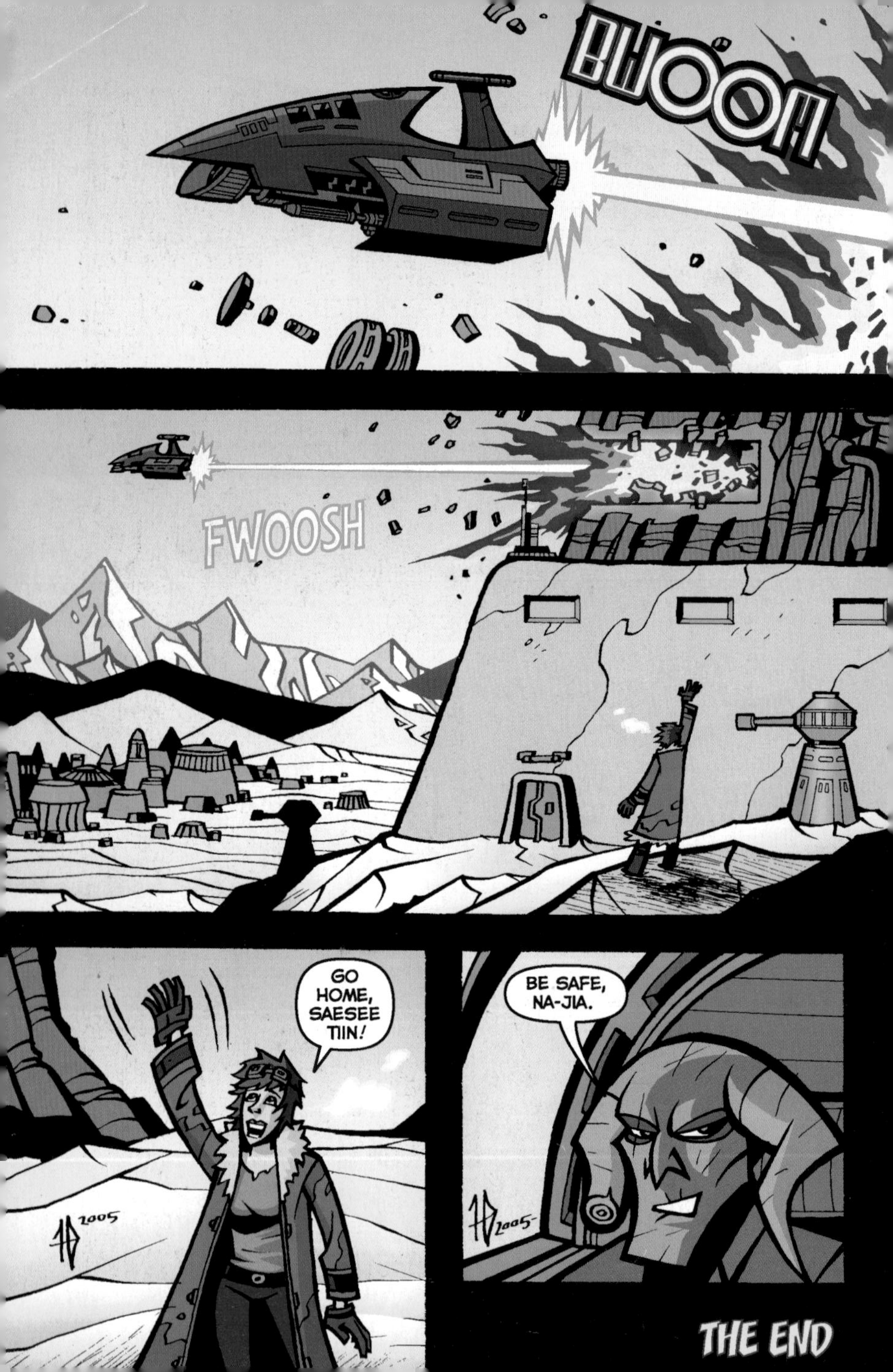
BWOOM
FWOOSH
GO HOME, SAESEE TIIN!
BE SAFE, NA-JIA.
THE END

EMERGENCY RE-ROUTING TO YORN SKOT, RESPONDING TO A DISTRESS CALL FROM JEDI TREETOWER.

H.O.P.E. SQUAD IN THE DROP A CLONE WARS ADVENTURE

TREETOWER HAD BEEN SENT TO RETRIEVE A SHIPMENT OF GOODS BEING SMUGGLED TO TRADE FEDERATION SEPARATISTS.

BUT SOMETHING WENT WRONG.

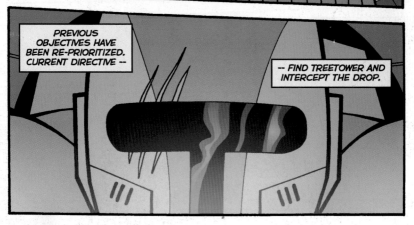

PREVIOUS OBJECTIVES HAVE BEEN RE-PRIORITIZED. CURRENT DIRECTIVE --

-- FIND TREETOWER AND INTERCEPT THE DROP.

THE NATURE OF THE SHIPMENT REMAINS UNKNOWN...

...BUT TREETOWER WAS ADAMANT ABOUT PURSUING THIS DELIVERY HIMSELF...

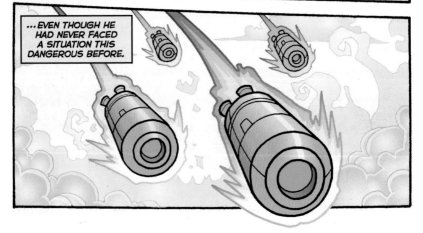

...EVEN THOUGH HE HAD NEVER FACED A SITUATION THIS DANGEROUS BEFORE.

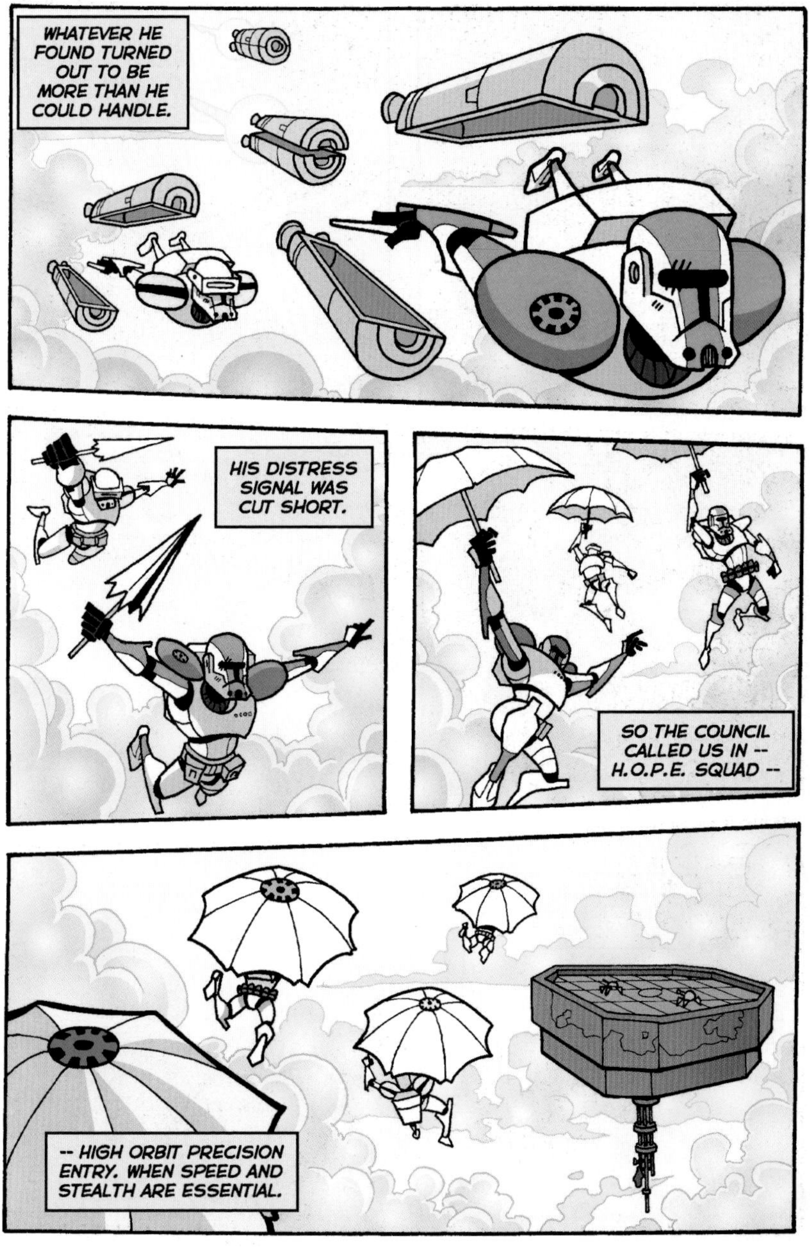
WHATEVER HE FOUND TURNED OUT TO BE MORE THAN HE COULD HANDLE.
HIS DISTRESS SIGNAL WAS CUT SHORT.
SO THE COUNCIL CALLED US IN -- H.O.P.E. SQUAD --
-- HIGH ORBIT PRECISION ENTRY. WHEN SPEED AND STEALTH ARE ESSENTIAL.

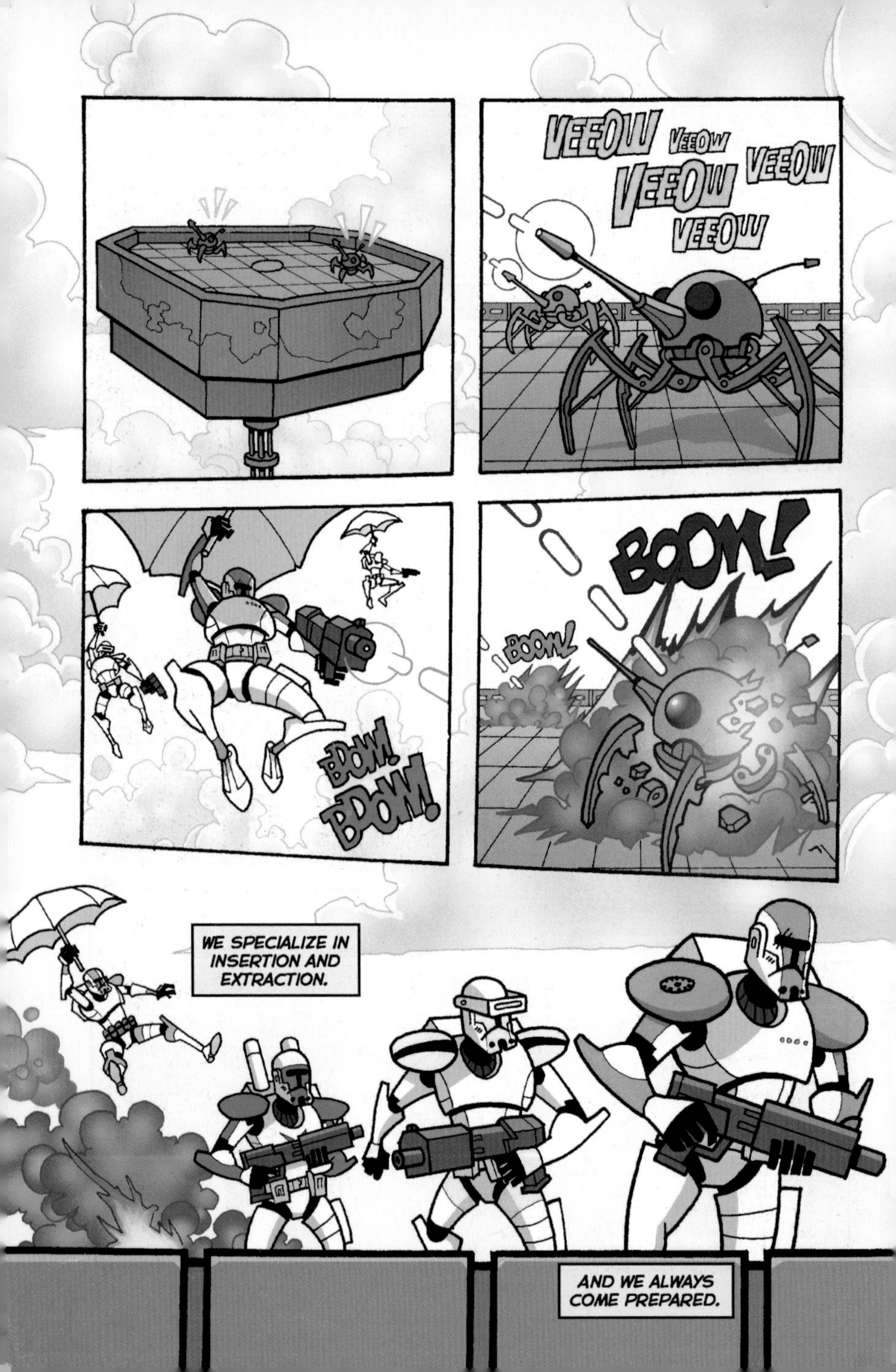
VEEOW
VEEOW
VEEOW
VEEOW
VEEOW
BDOM!
BDOM!
BOOM!
BOOM!
WE SPECIALIZE IN INSERTION AND EXTRACTION.
AND WE ALWAYS COME PREPARED.

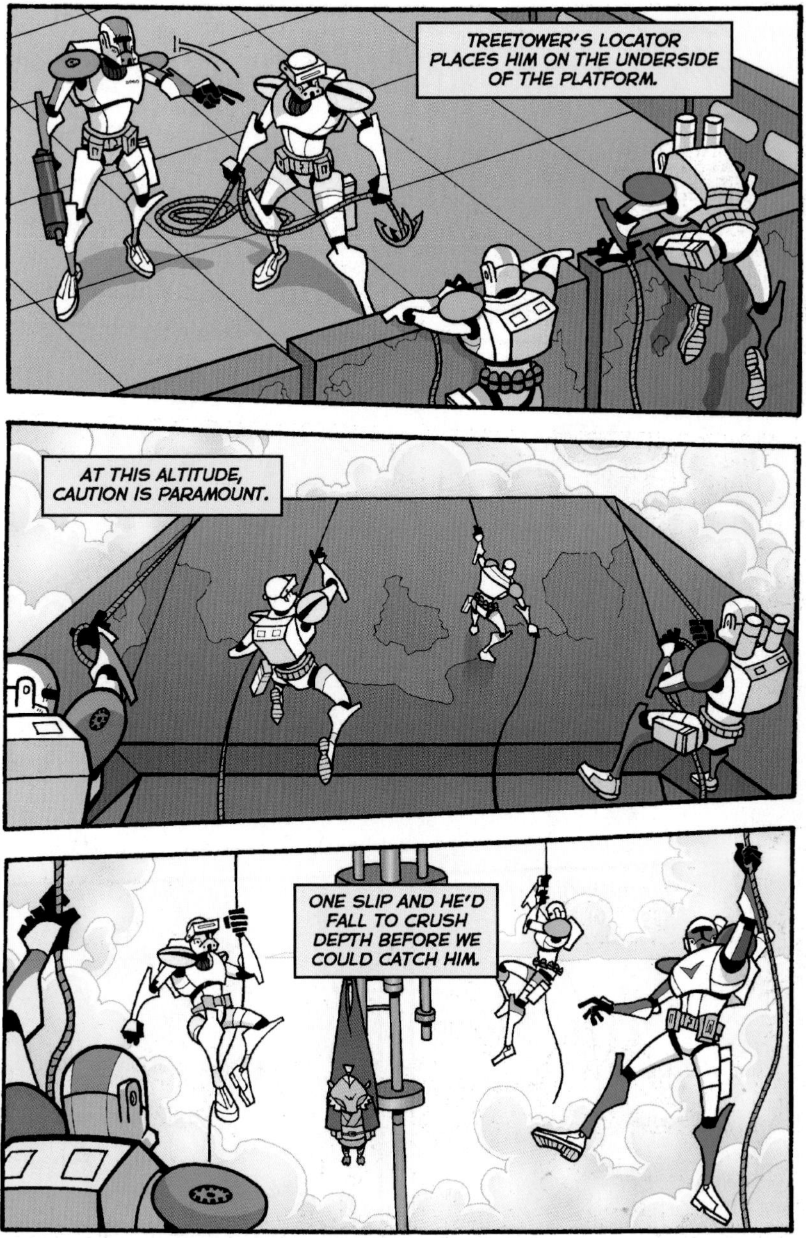
TREETOWER'S LOCATOR PLACES HIM ON THE UNDERSIDE OF THE PLATFORM.
AT THIS ALTITUDE, CAUTION IS PARAMOUNT.
ONE SLIP AND HE'D FALL TO CRUSH DEPTH BEFORE WE COULD CATCH HIM.

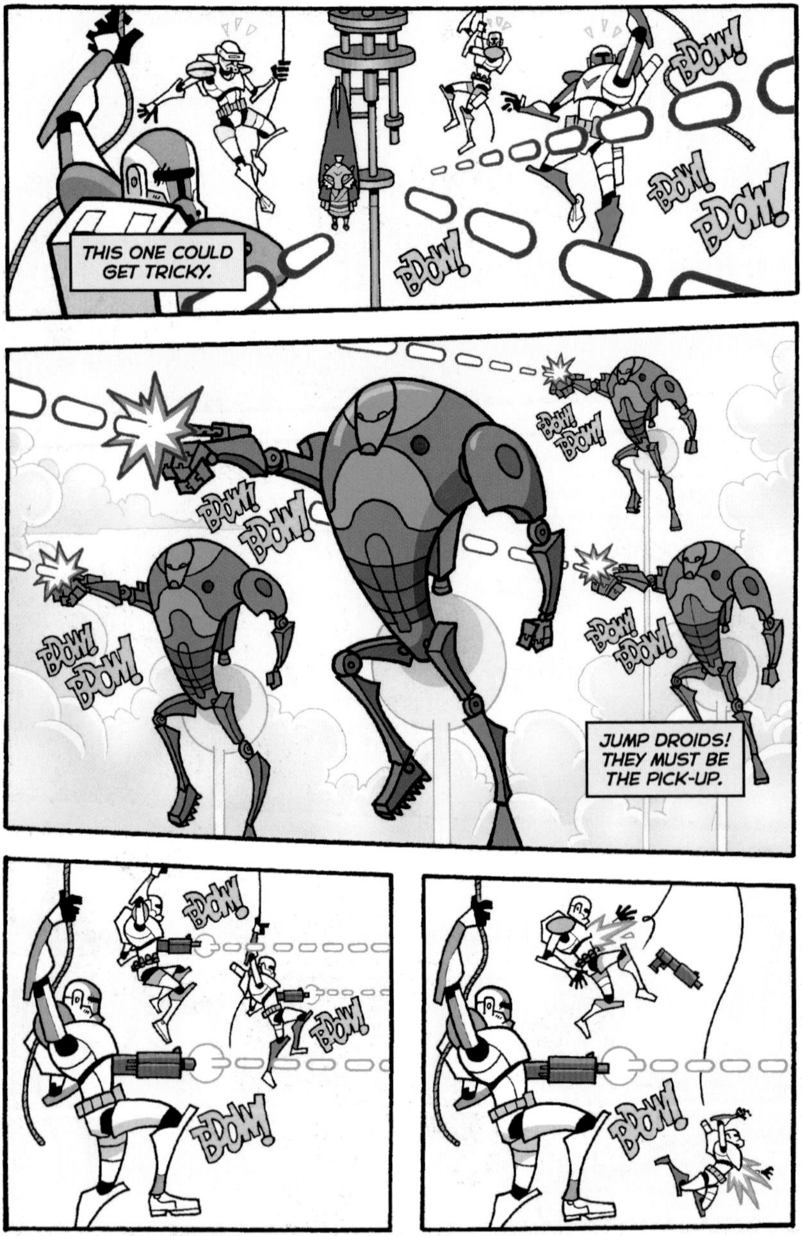
BDOW!
BDOW!
BDOW!
BDOW!
THIS ONE COULD GET TRICKY.
BDOW!
BDOW!
BDOW!
BDOW!
BDOW!
BDOW!
BDOW!
BDOW!
JUMP DROIDS! THEY MUST BE THE PICK-UP.
BDOW!
BDOW!
BDOW!
BDOW!

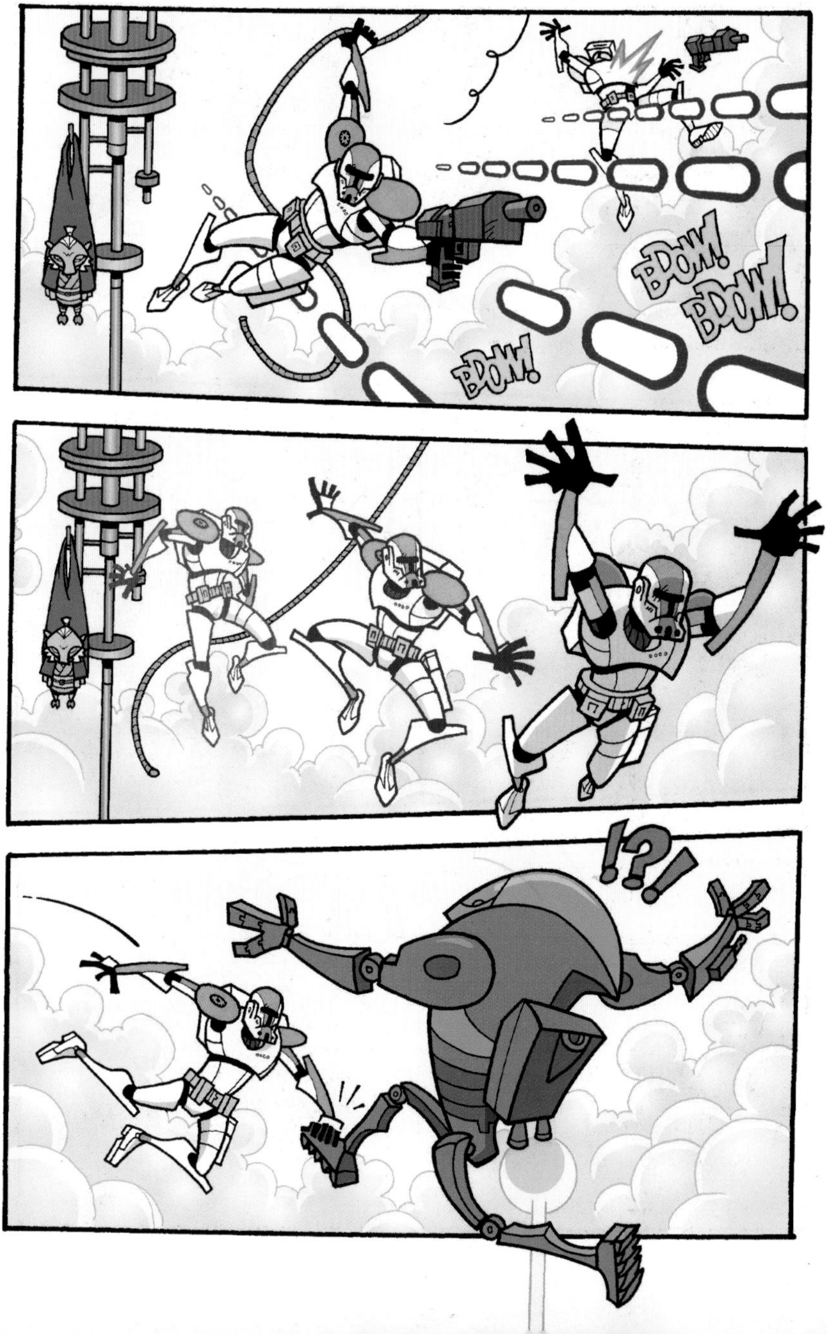
BDOW!
BDOW!
BDOW!
!?!

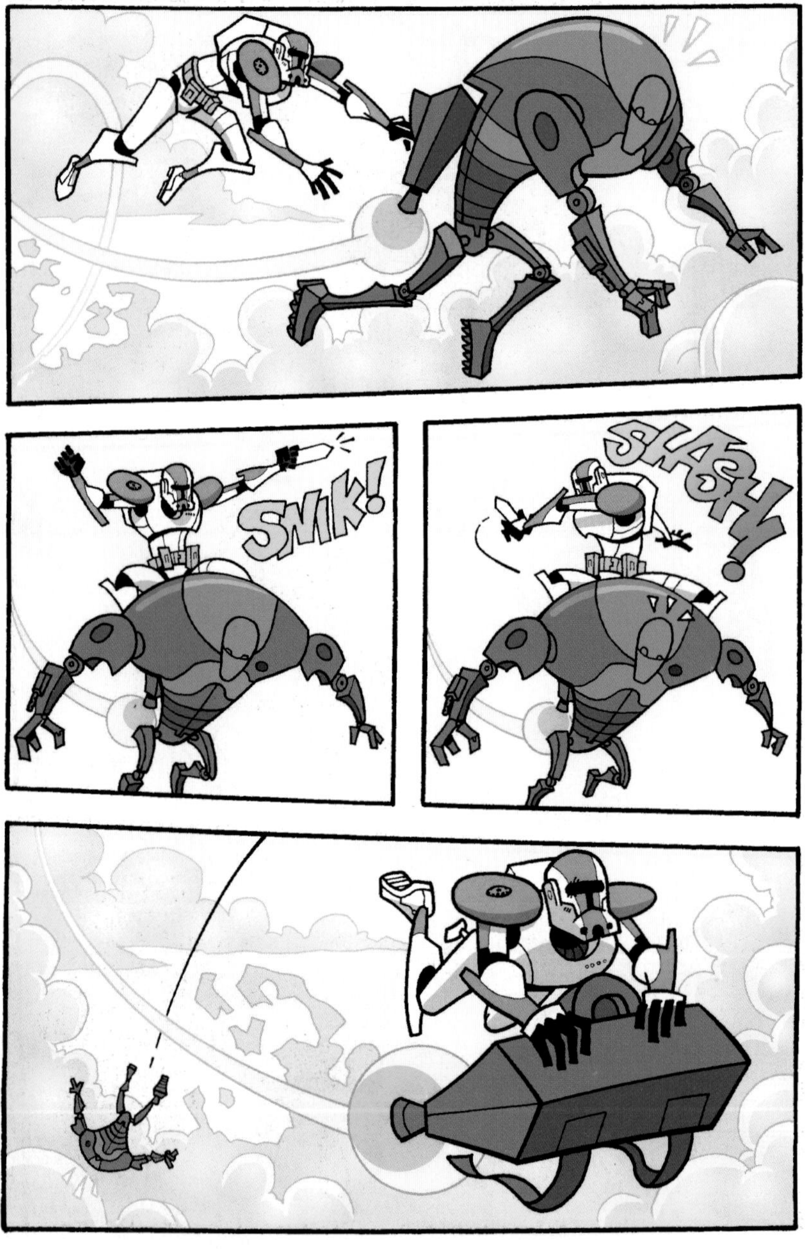
SNIK!
SHASH!

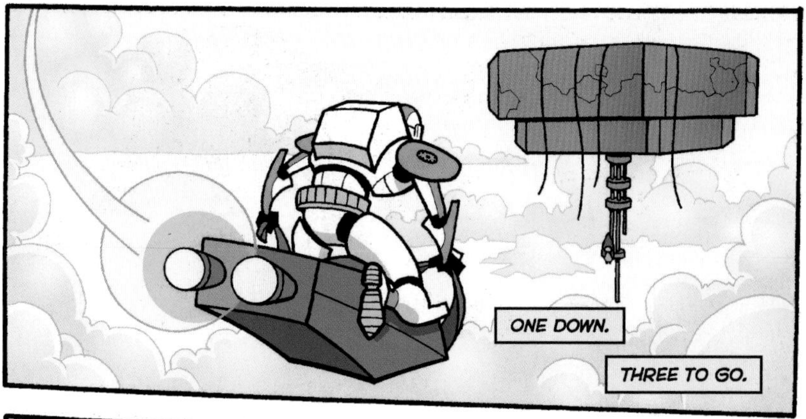
ONE DOWN.
THREE TO GO.

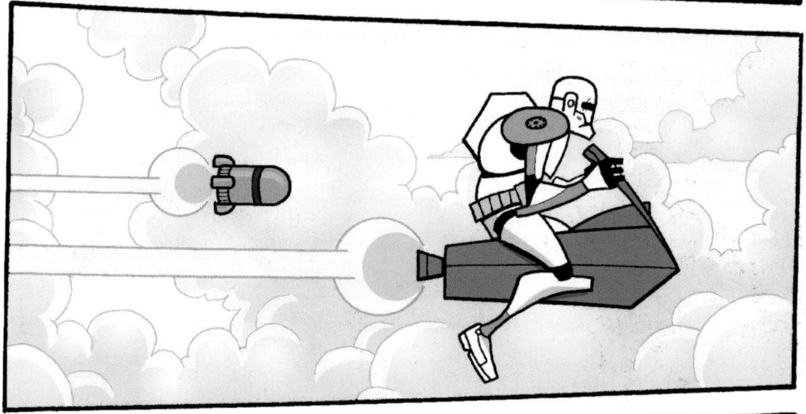

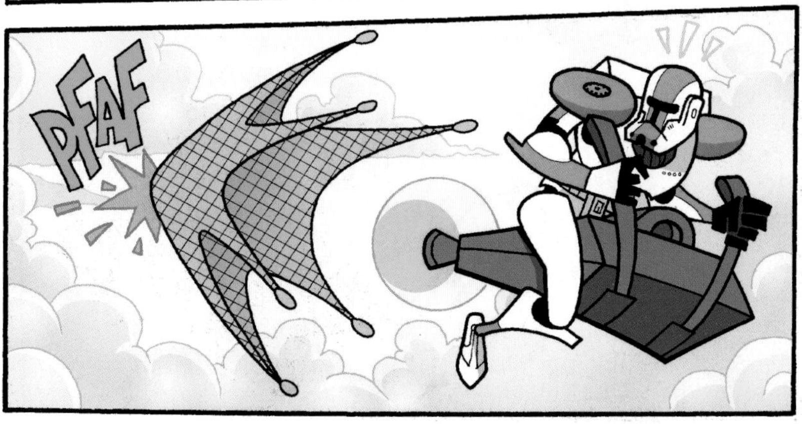
PFAF

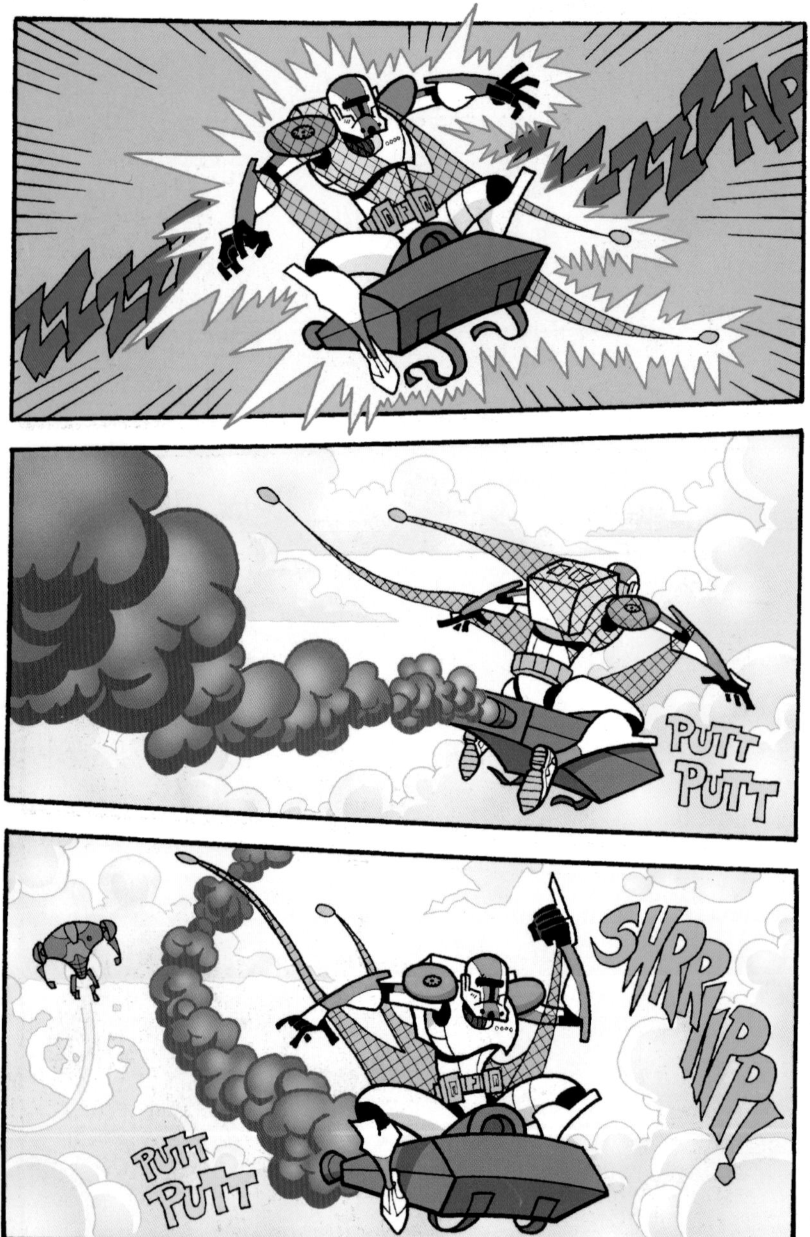
ZZZZZ
ZZZZZAP
PUTT PUTT
SHRRIPP!
PUTT PUTT

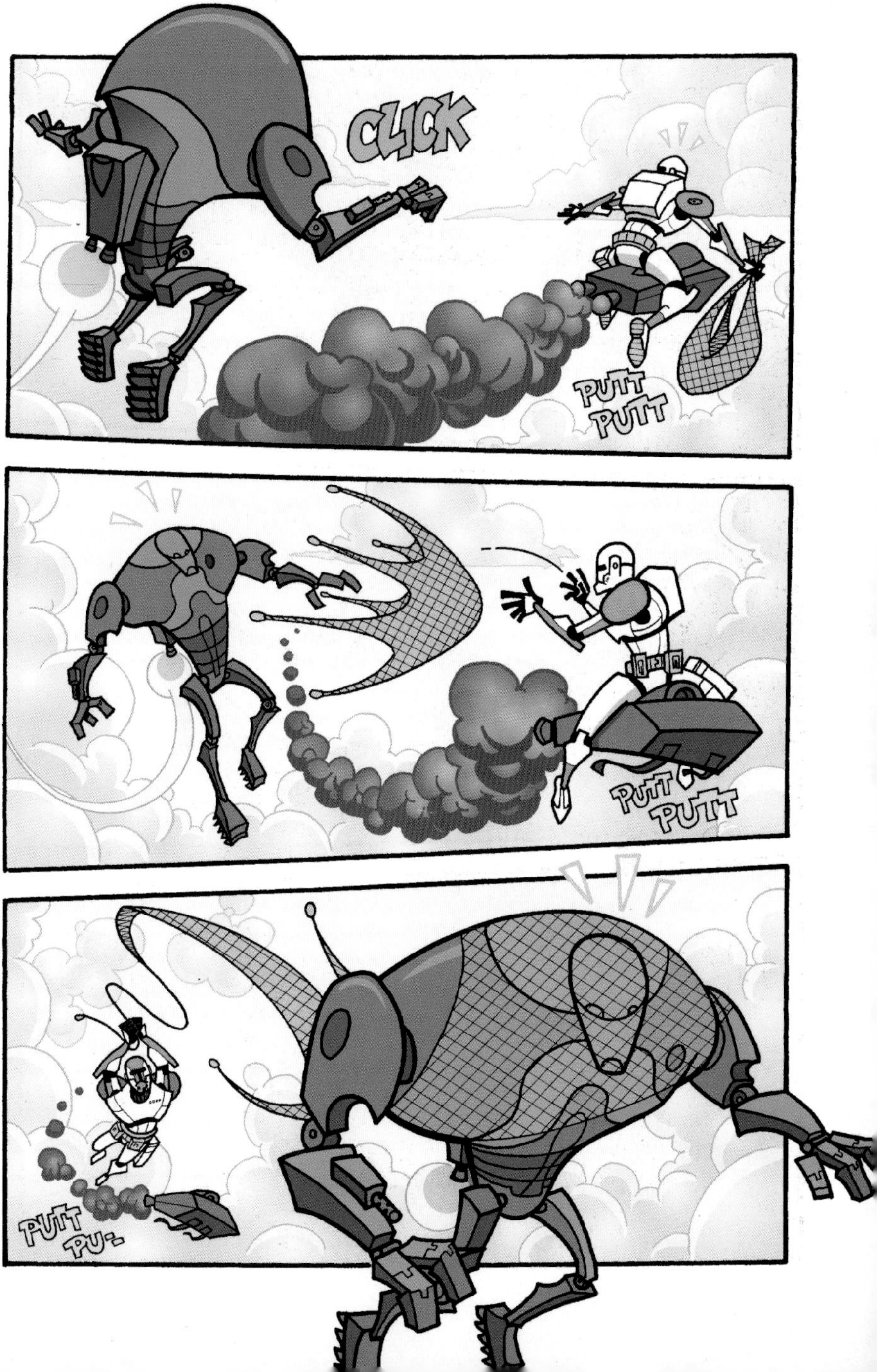
CLICK
PUTT
PUTT
PUTT
PUTT
PUTT
PU-

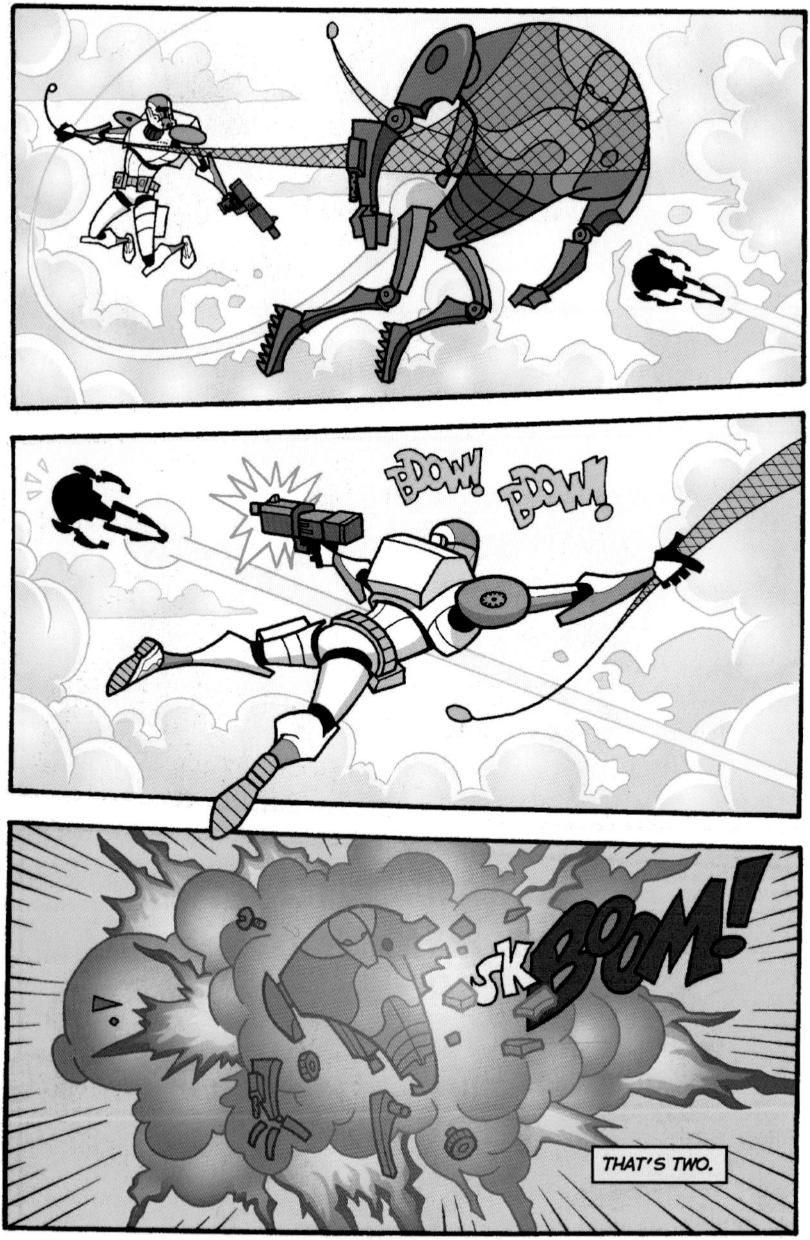
BDOW!
BDOW!
SKBOOM!
THAT'S TWO.

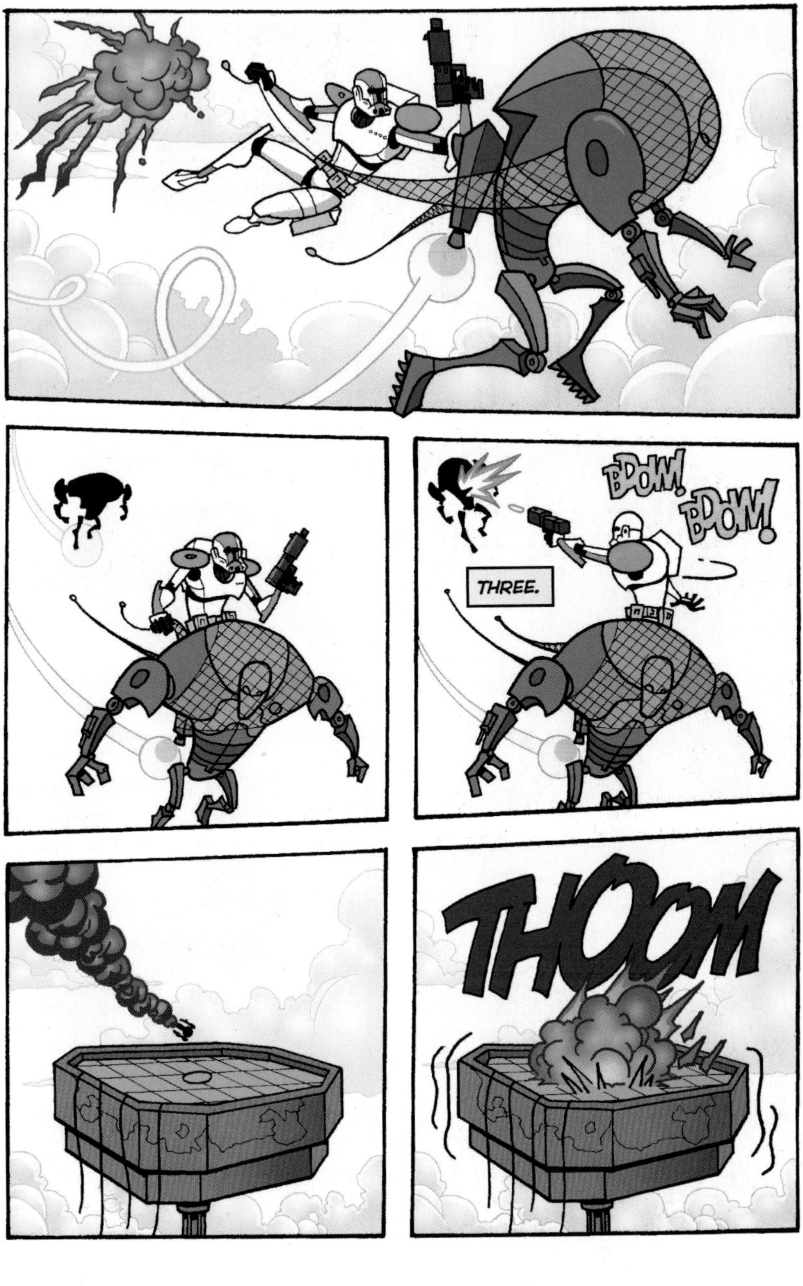
BDOW!
BDOW!
THREE.
THOOM

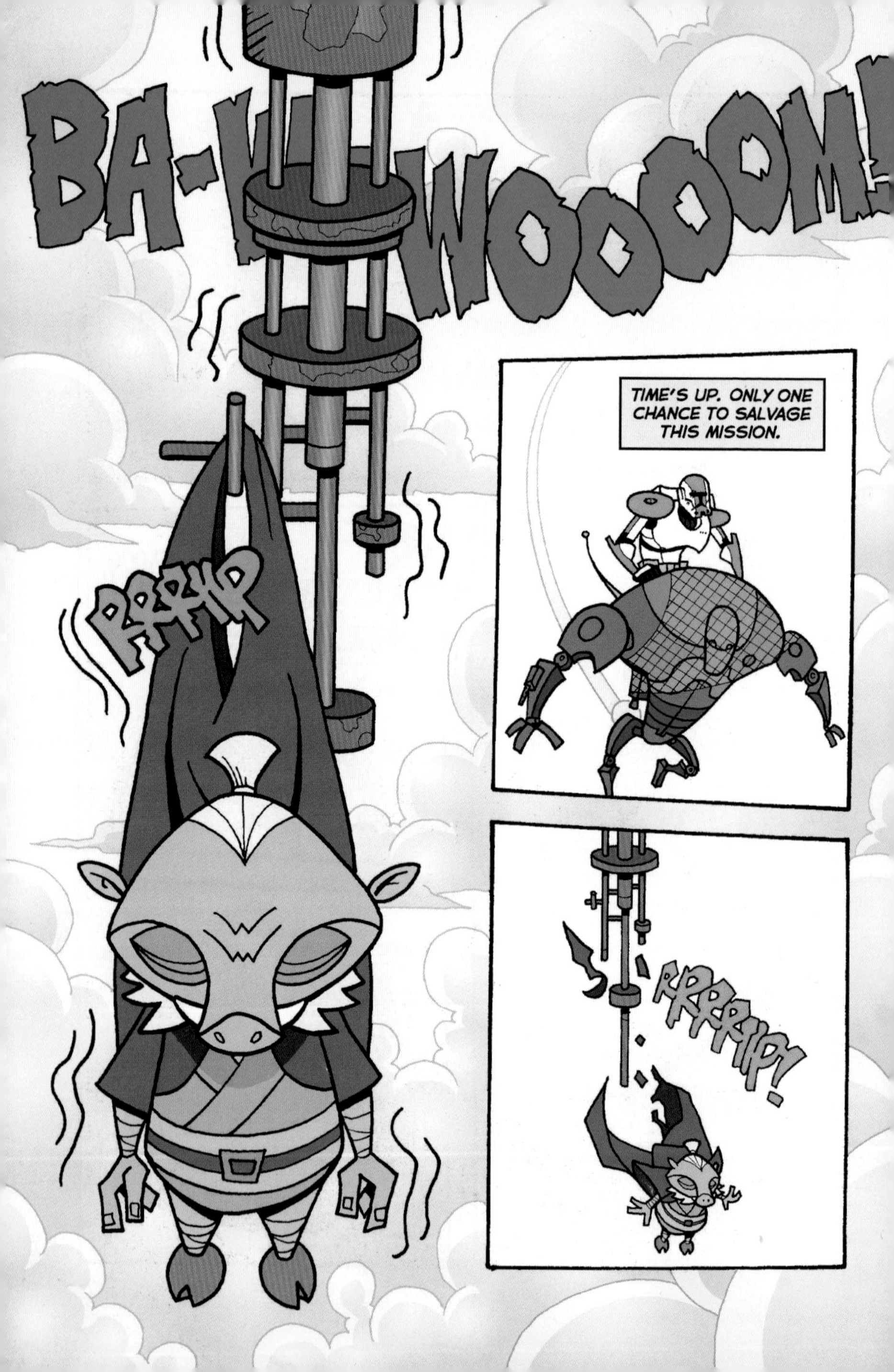
BA-WHOOOOM!
RRRIP
TIME'S UP. ONLY ONE CHANCE TO SALVAGE THIS MISSION.
RRRRIP!

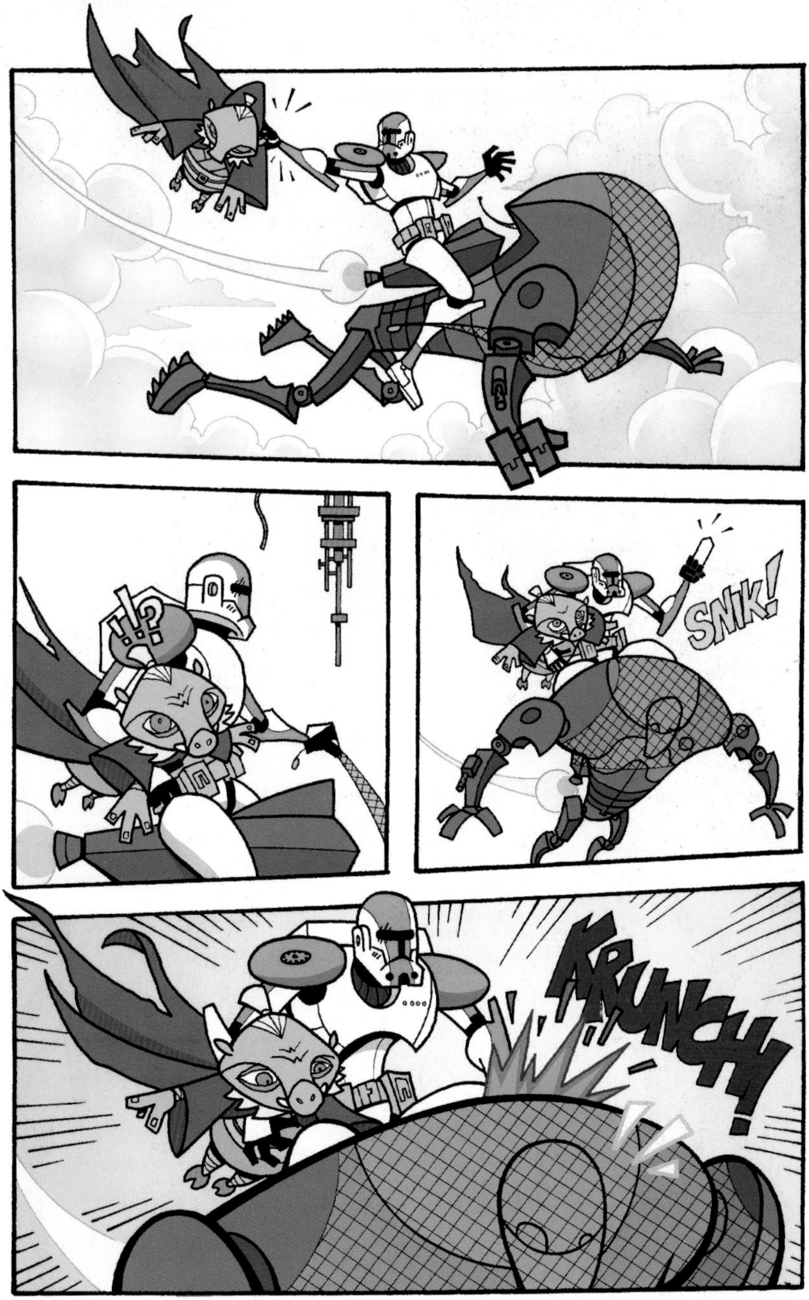
!?
SNIK!
KRUNCH!

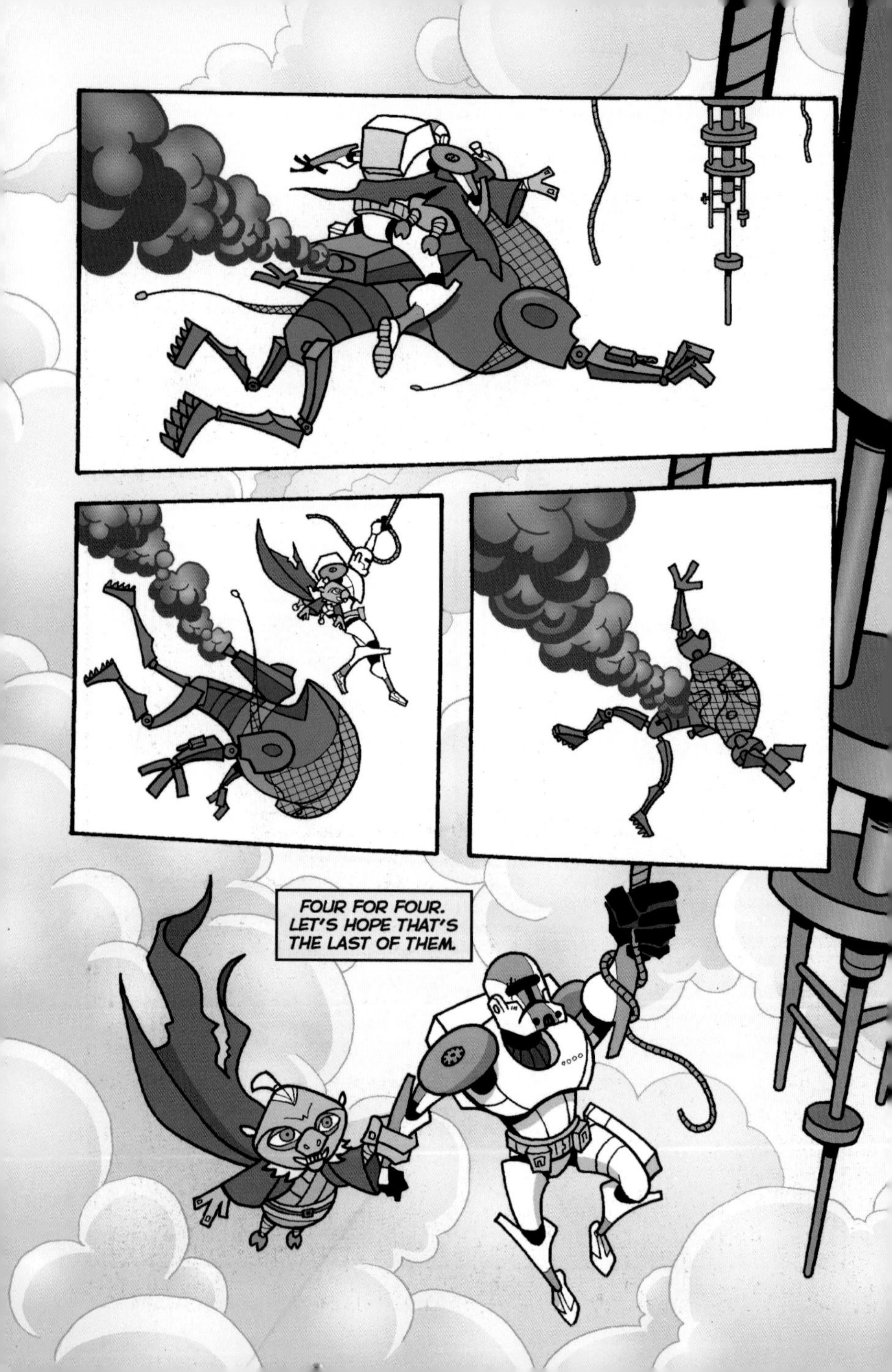
FOUR FOR FOUR.
LET'S HOPE THAT'S
THE LAST OF THEM.

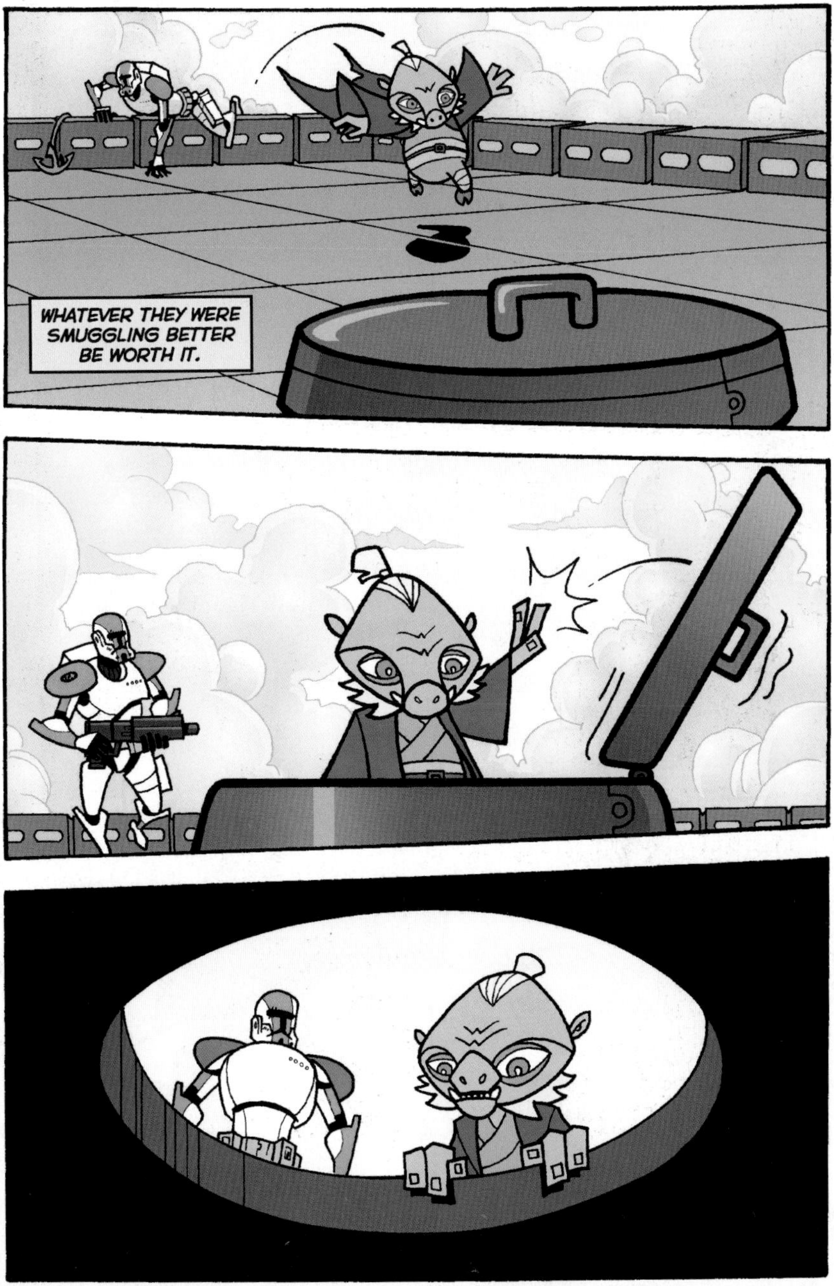
WHATEVER THEY WERE SMUGGLING BETTER BE WORTH IT.

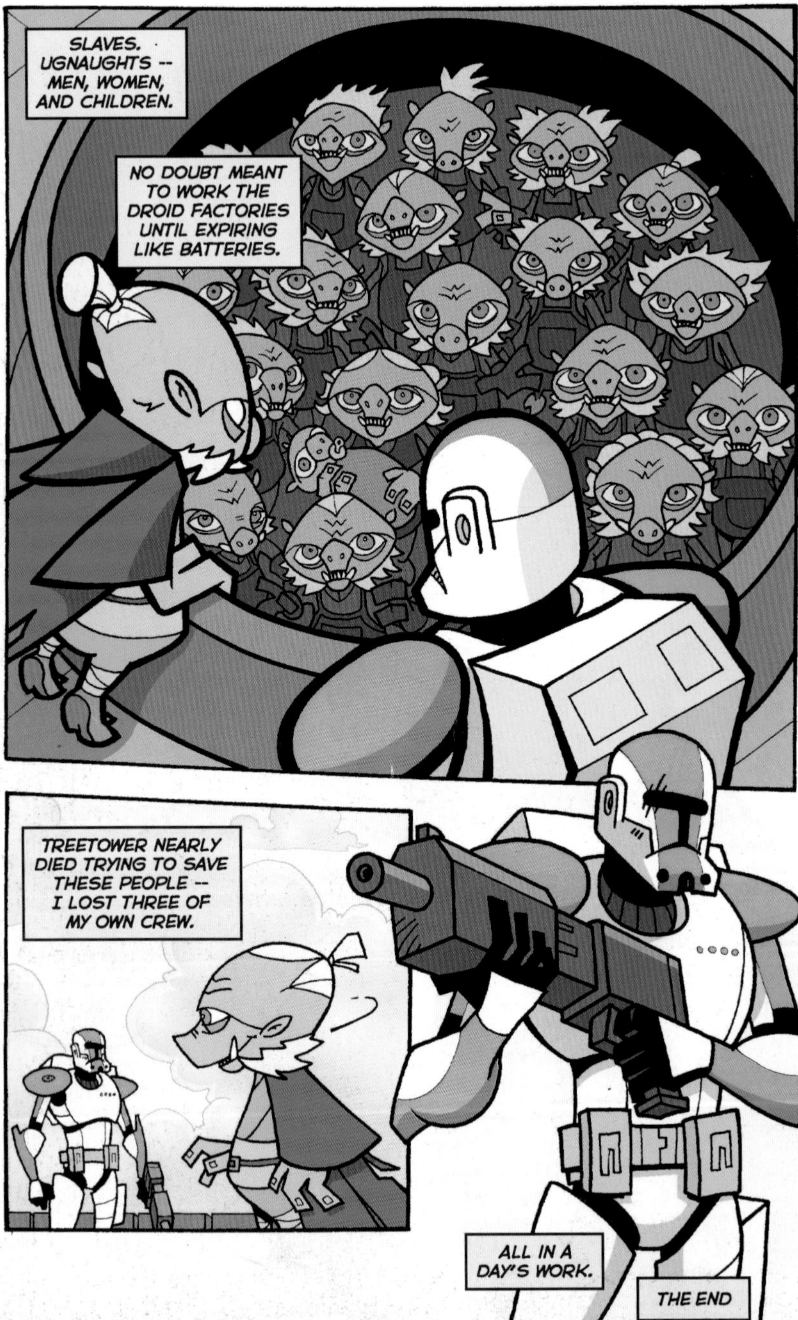
SLAVES. UGNAUGHTS -- MEN, WOMEN, AND CHILDREN.
NO DOUBT MEANT TO WORK THE DROID FACTORIES UNTIL EXPIRING LIKE BATTERIES.
TREETOWER NEARLY DIED TRYING TO SAVE THESE PEOPLE -- I LOST THREE OF MY OWN CREW.
ALL IN A DAY'S WORK.
THE END

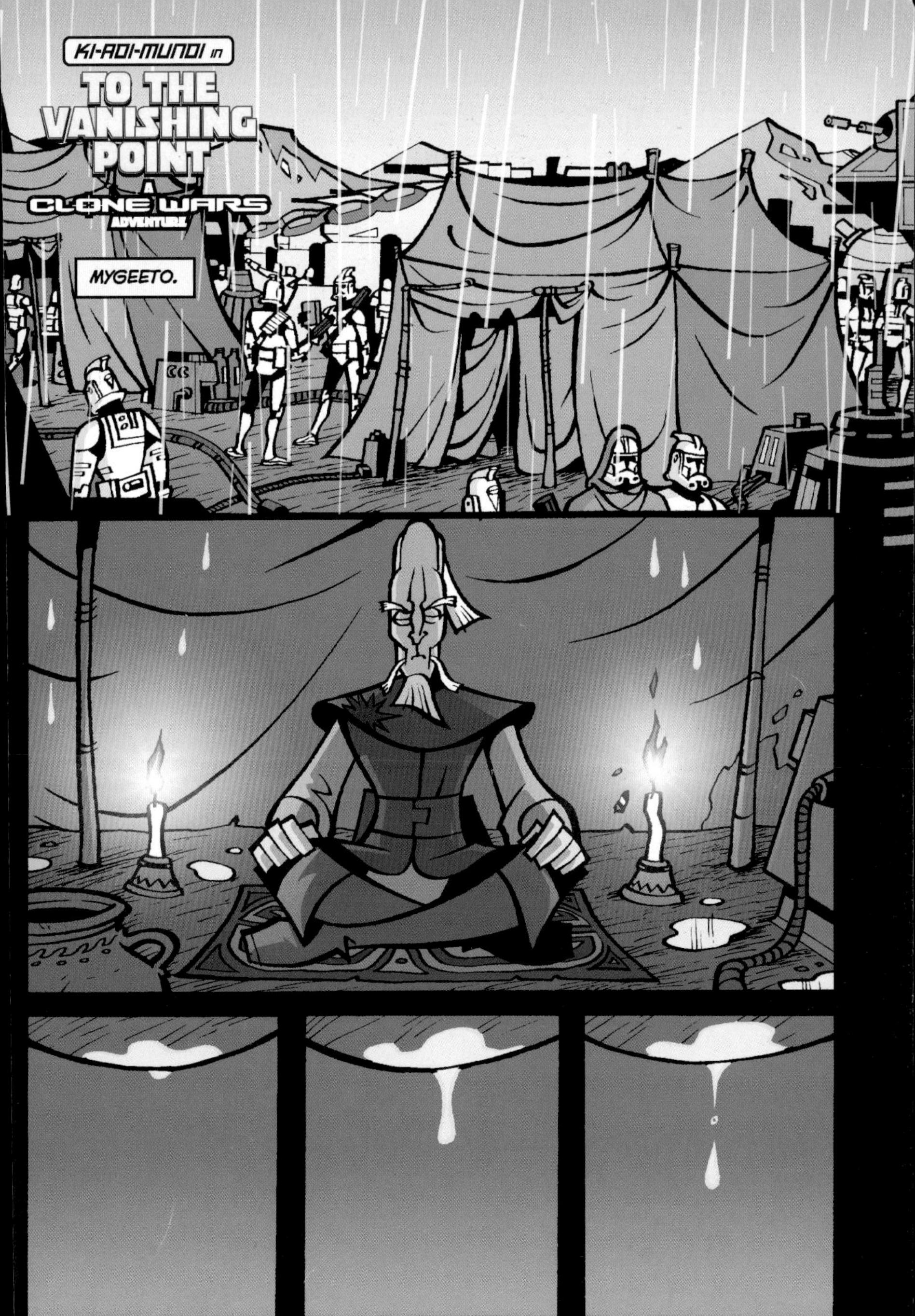
KI-ADI-MUNDI in
TO THE VANISHING POINT
A CLONE WARS ADVENTURE
MYGEETO.

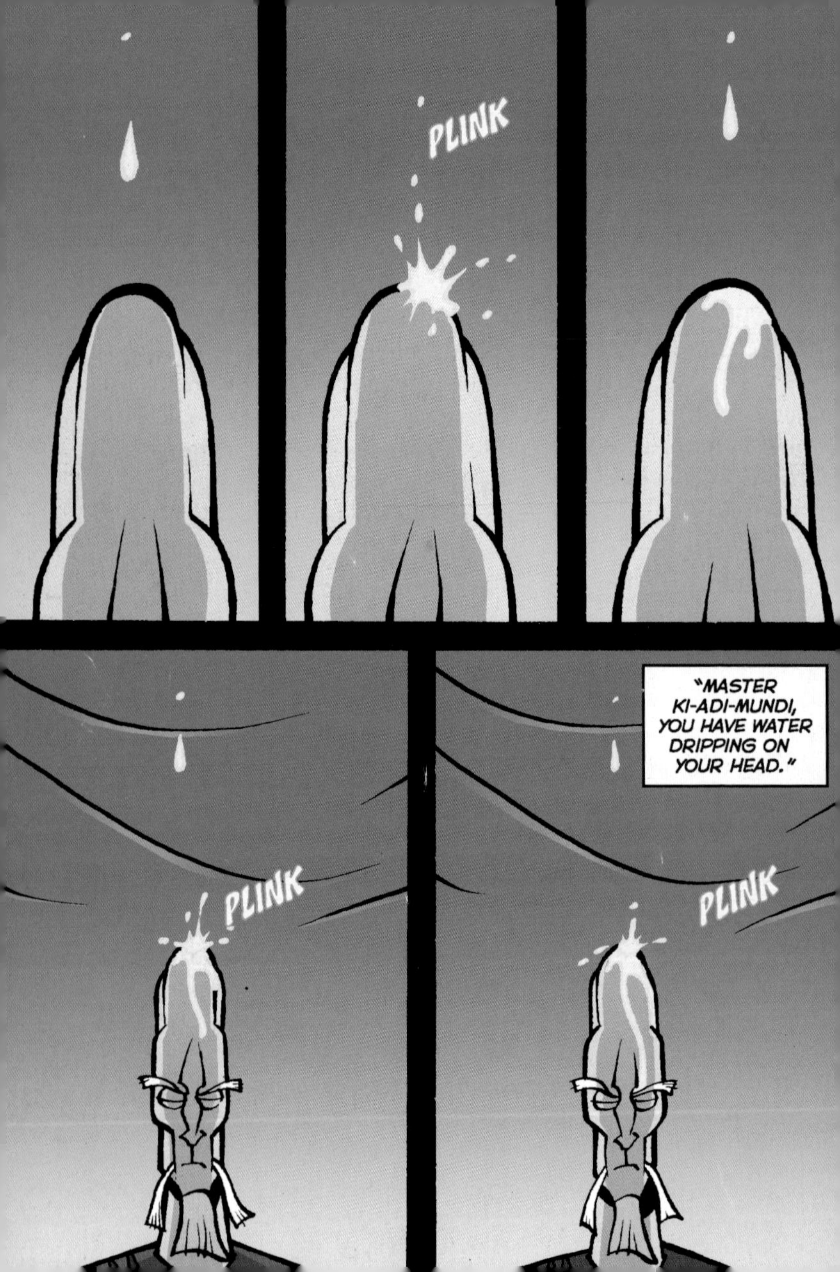
PLINK
PLINK
"MASTER KI-ADI-MUNDI, YOU HAVE WATER DRIPPING ON YOUR HEAD."
PLINK

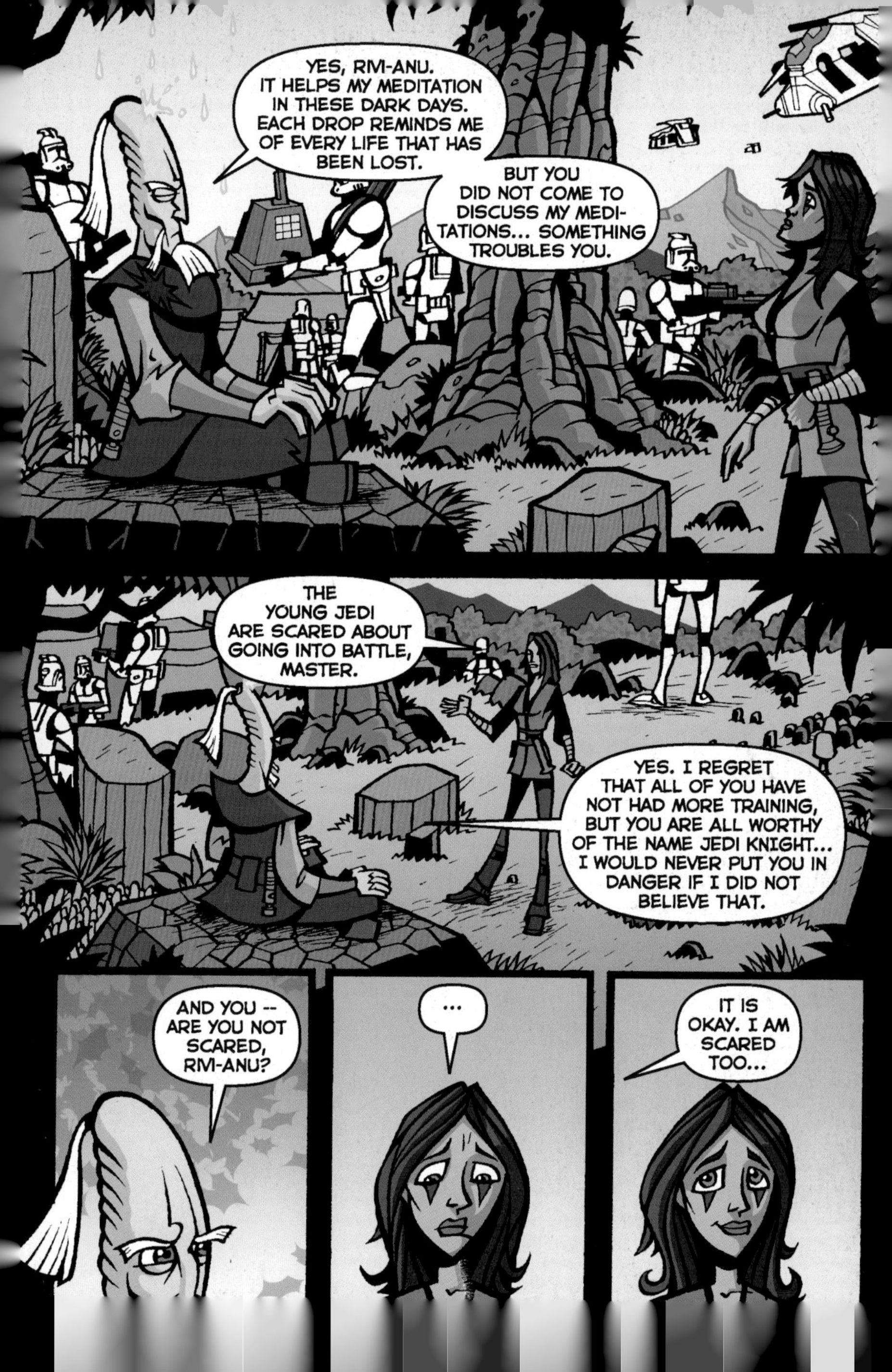
YES, RIVI-ANU. IT HELPS MY MEDITATION IN THESE DARK DAYS. EACH DROP REMINDS ME OF EVERY LIFE THAT HAS BEEN LOST.
BUT YOU DID NOT COME TO DISCUSS MY MEDITATIONS... SOMETHING TROUBLES YOU.
THE YOUNG JEDI ARE SCARED ABOUT GOING INTO BATTLE, MASTER.
YES. I REGRET THAT ALL OF YOU HAVE NOT HAD MORE TRAINING, BUT YOU ARE ALL WORTHY OF THE NAME JEDI KNIGHT... I WOULD NEVER PUT YOU IN DANGER IF I DID NOT BELIEVE THAT.
AND YOU -- ARE YOU NOT SCARED, RIVI-ANU?
...
IT IS OKAY. I AM SCARED TOO...

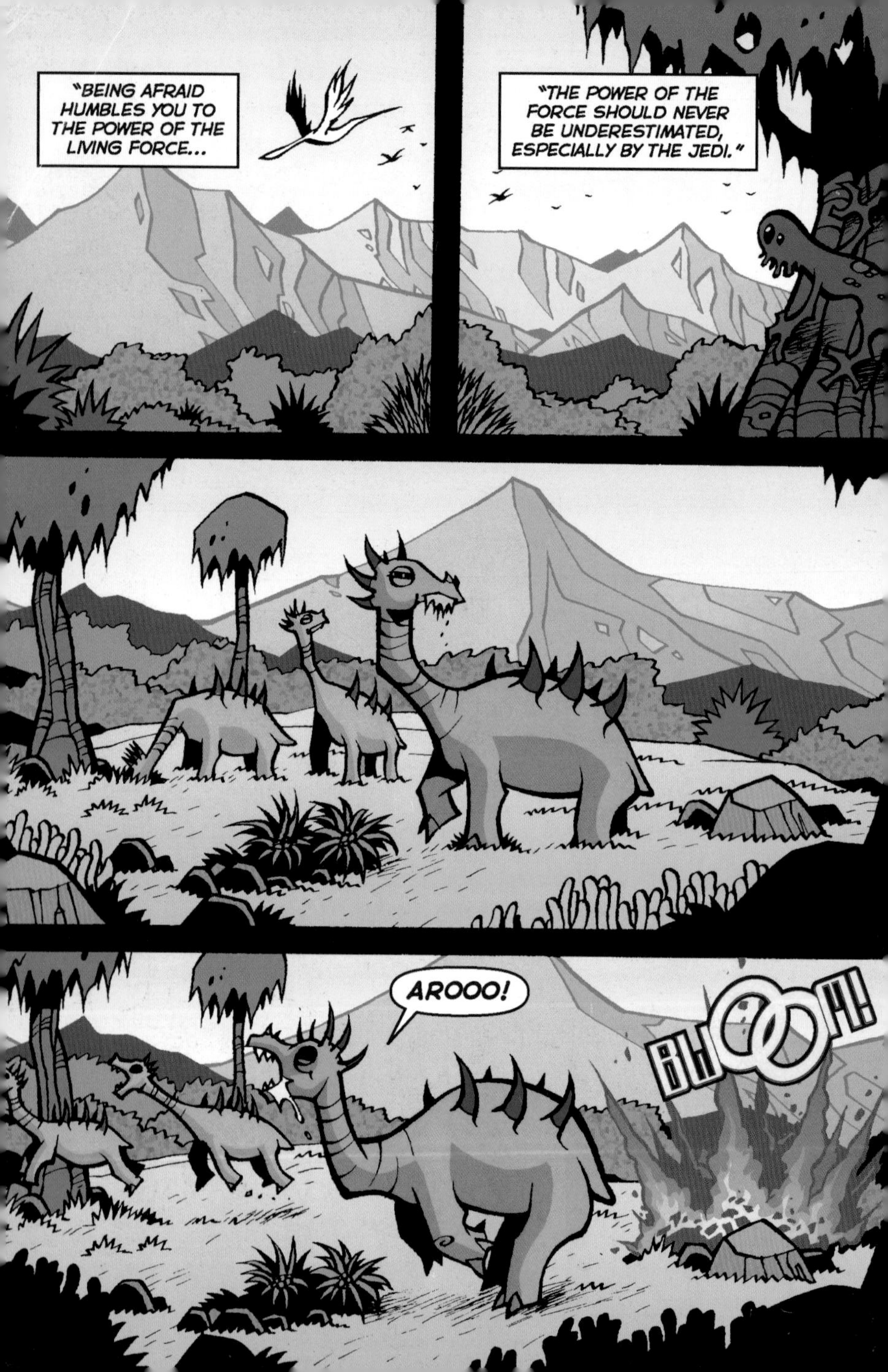
"BEING AFRAID HUMBLES YOU TO THE POWER OF THE LIVING FORCE...
"THE POWER OF THE FORCE SHOULD NEVER BE UNDERESTIMATED, ESPECIALLY BY THE JEDI."
AROOO!
BHOOM!

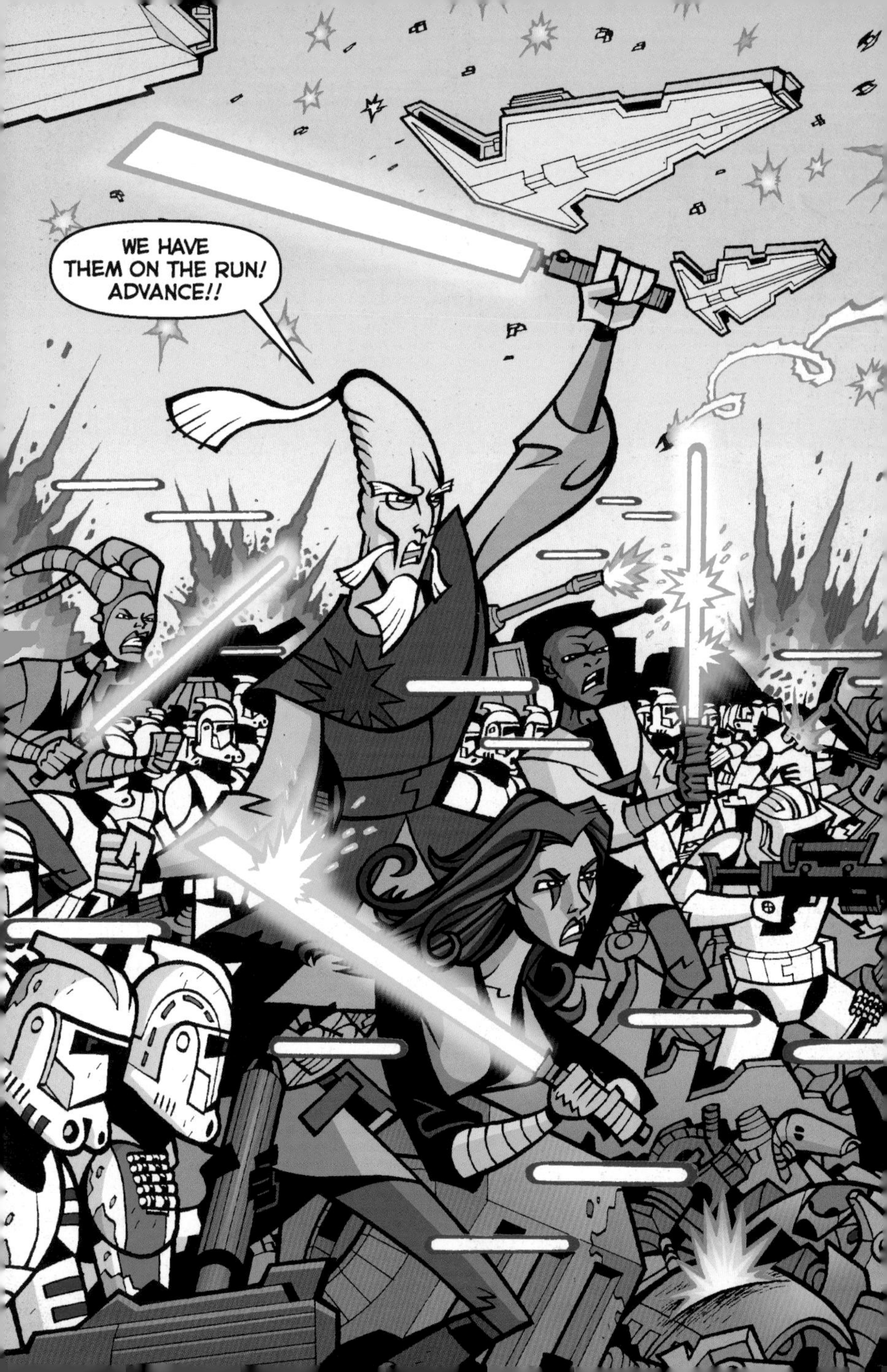
WE HAVE THEM ON THE RUN! ADVANCE!!

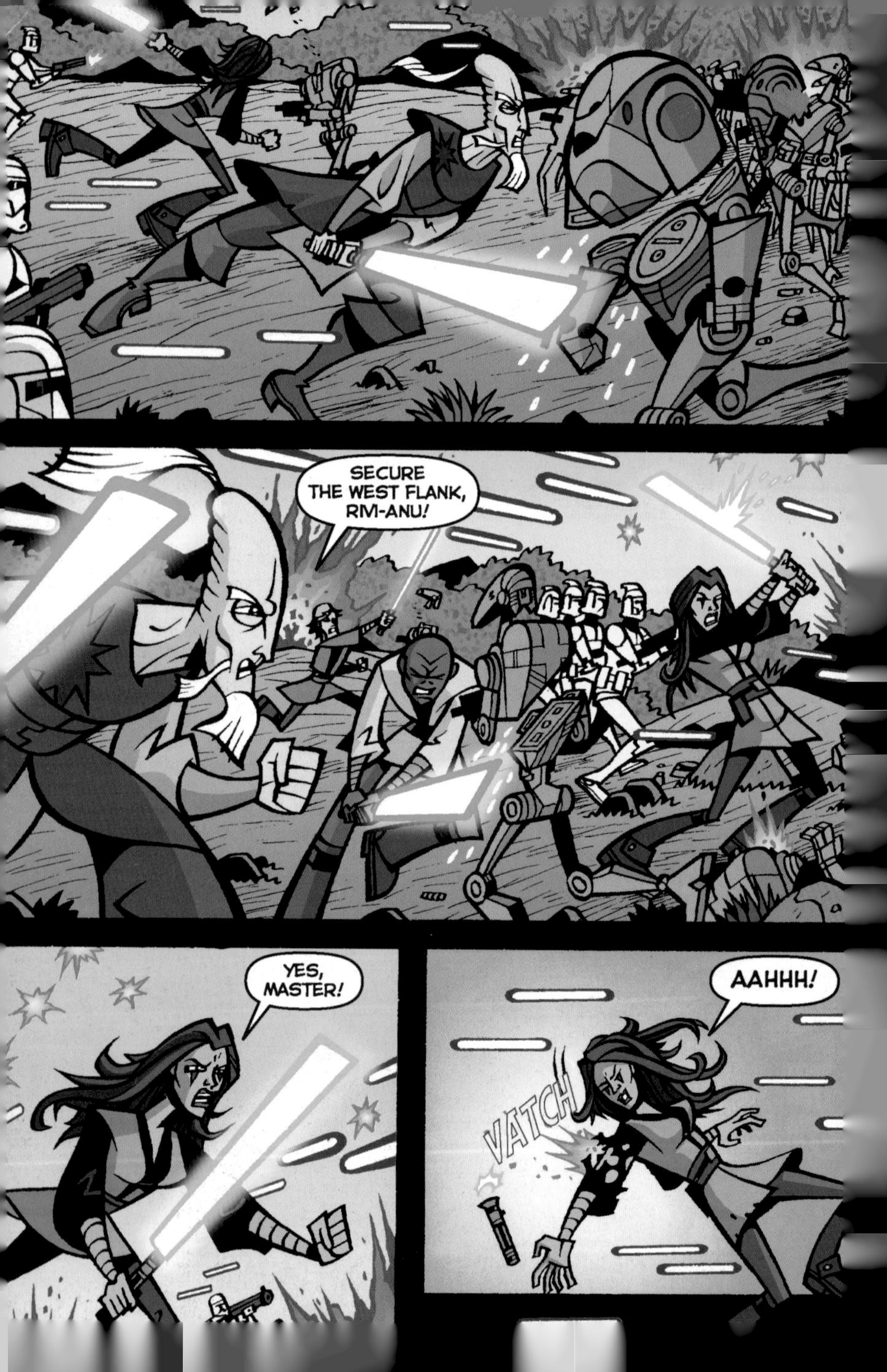
SECURE THE WEST FLANK, RIVI-ANU!
YES, MASTER!
AAHHH!
VATCH

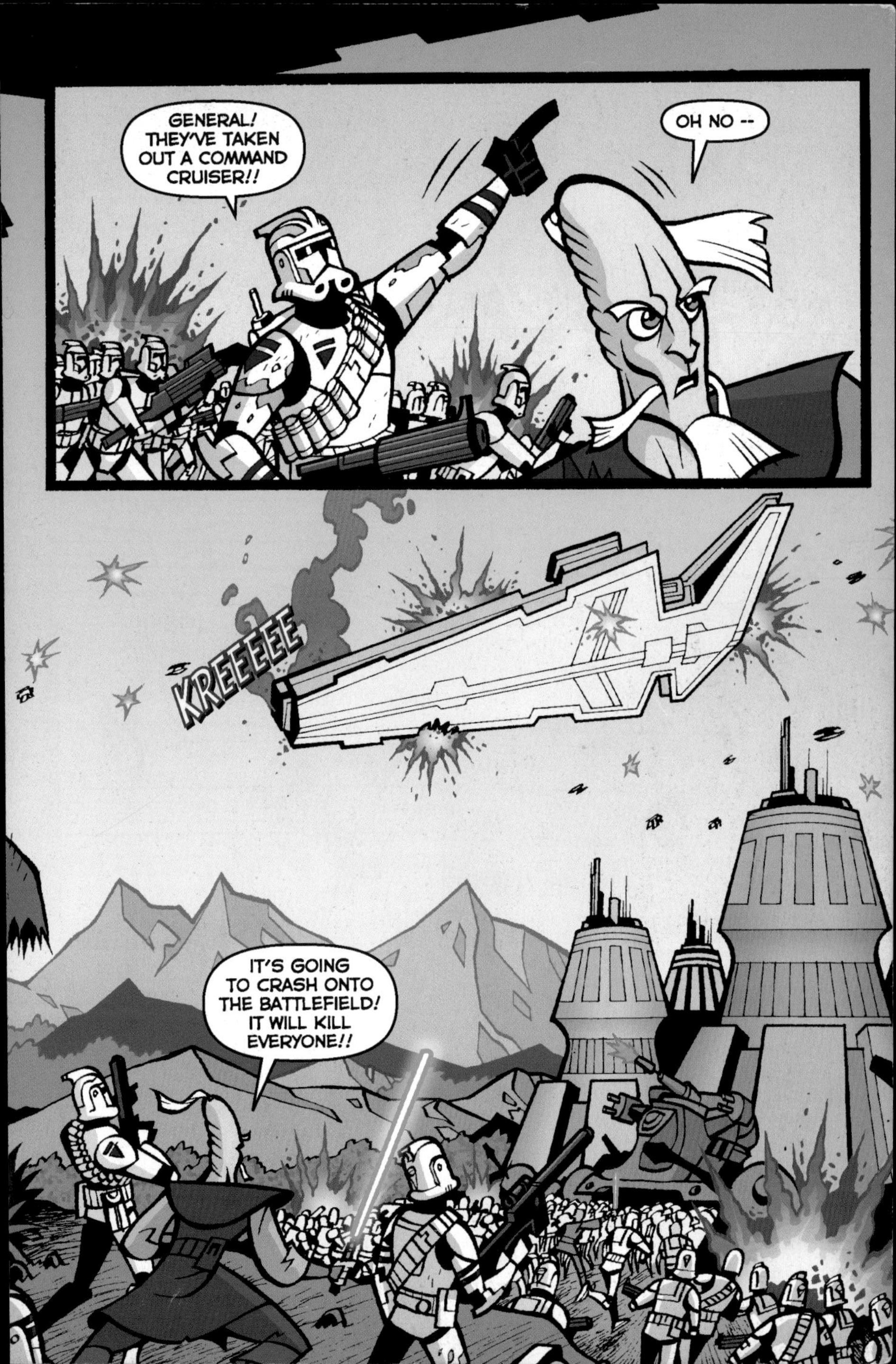
GENERAL! THEY'VE TAKEN OUT A COMMAND CRUISER!!
OH NO --
KREEEEEE
IT'S GOING TO CRASH ONTO THE BATTLEFIELD! IT WILL KILL EVERYONE!!

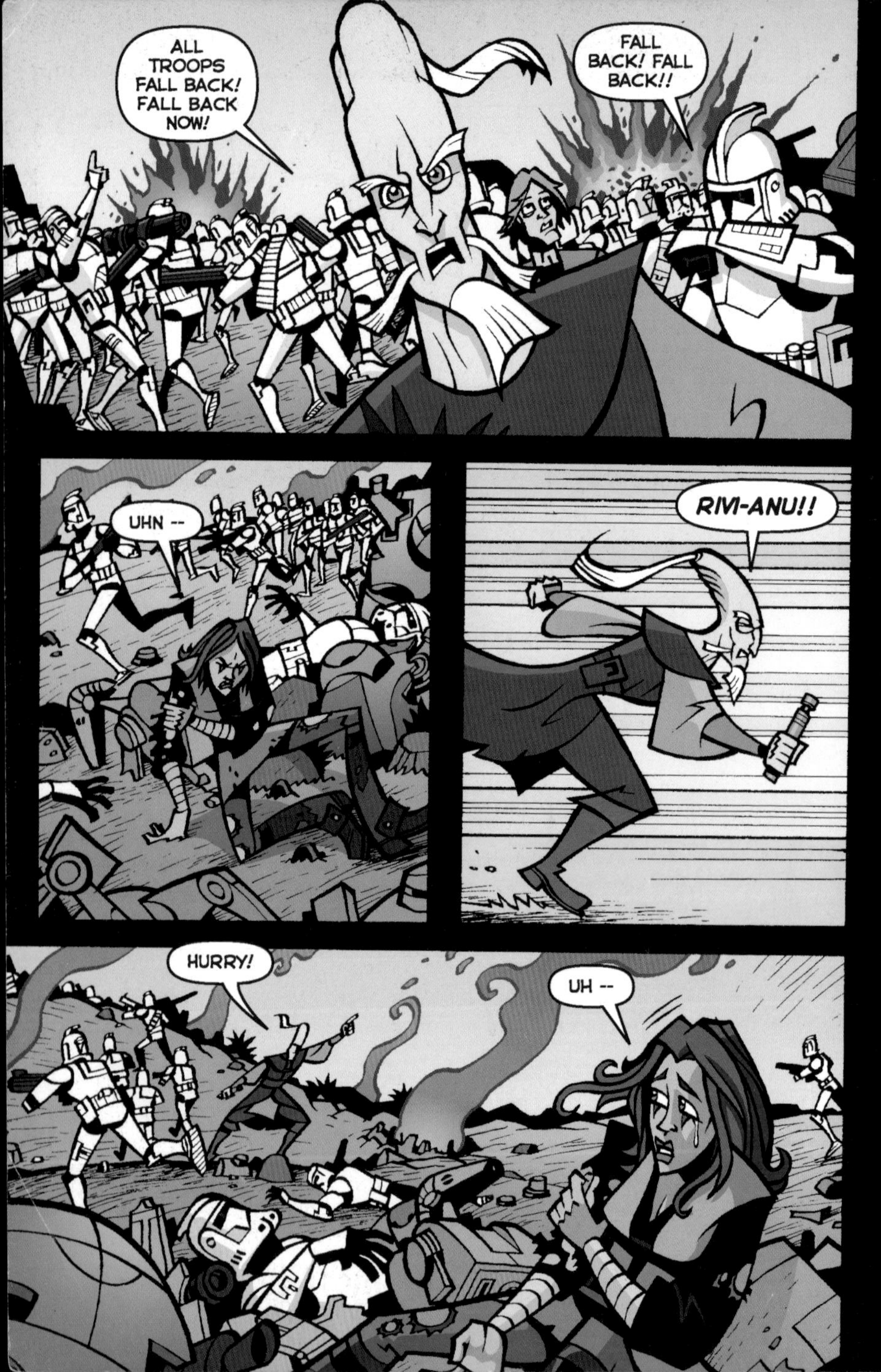
ALL TROOPS FALL BACK! FALL BACK NOW!
FALL BACK! FALL BACK!!
UHN --
RIVI-ANU!!
HURRY!
UH --

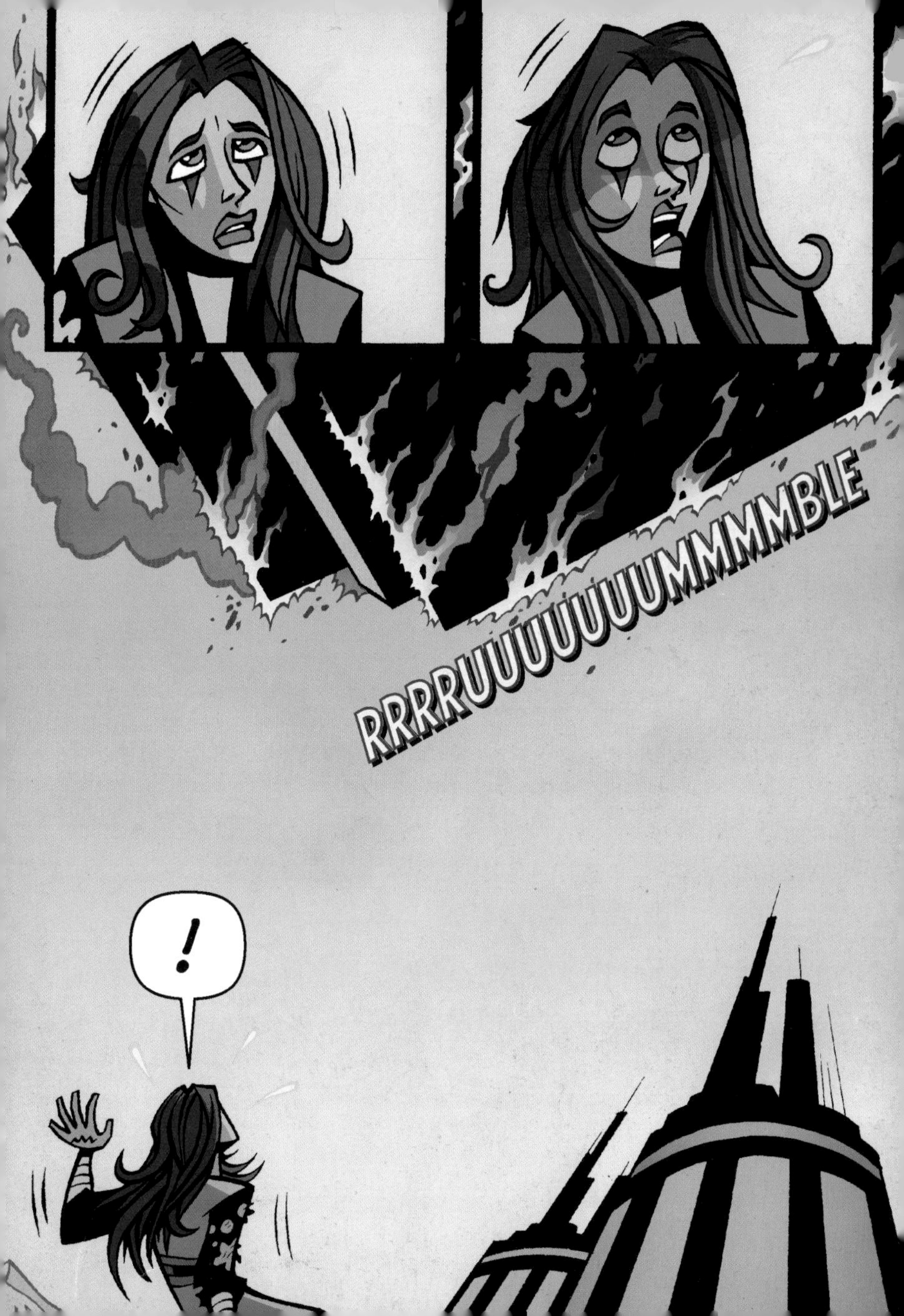
RRRRUUUUUUUUMMMMMBLE
!

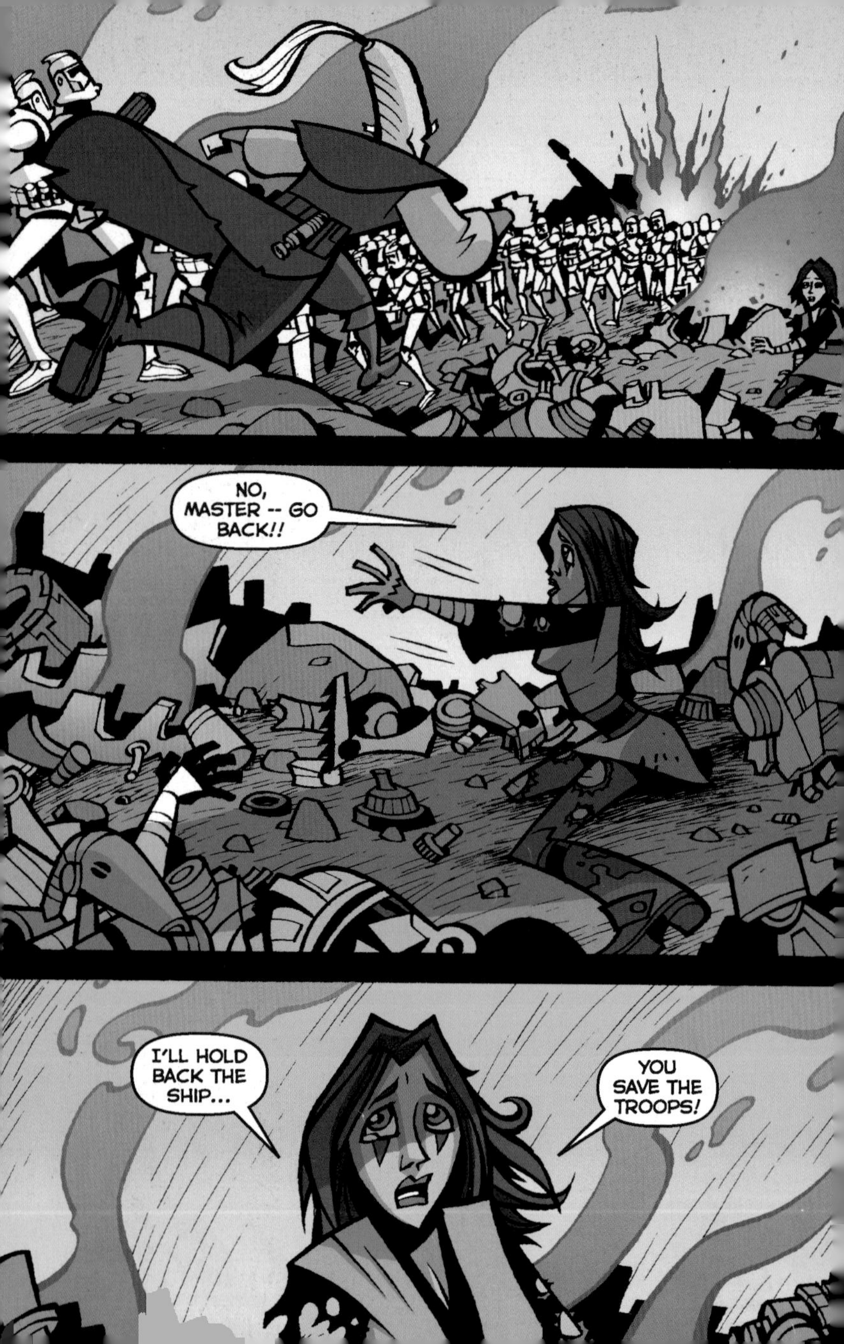
NO, MASTER -- GO BACK!!
I'LL HOLD BACK THE SHIP...
YOU SAVE THE TROOPS!

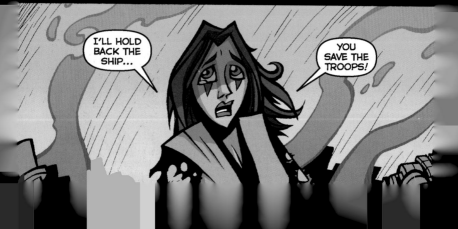

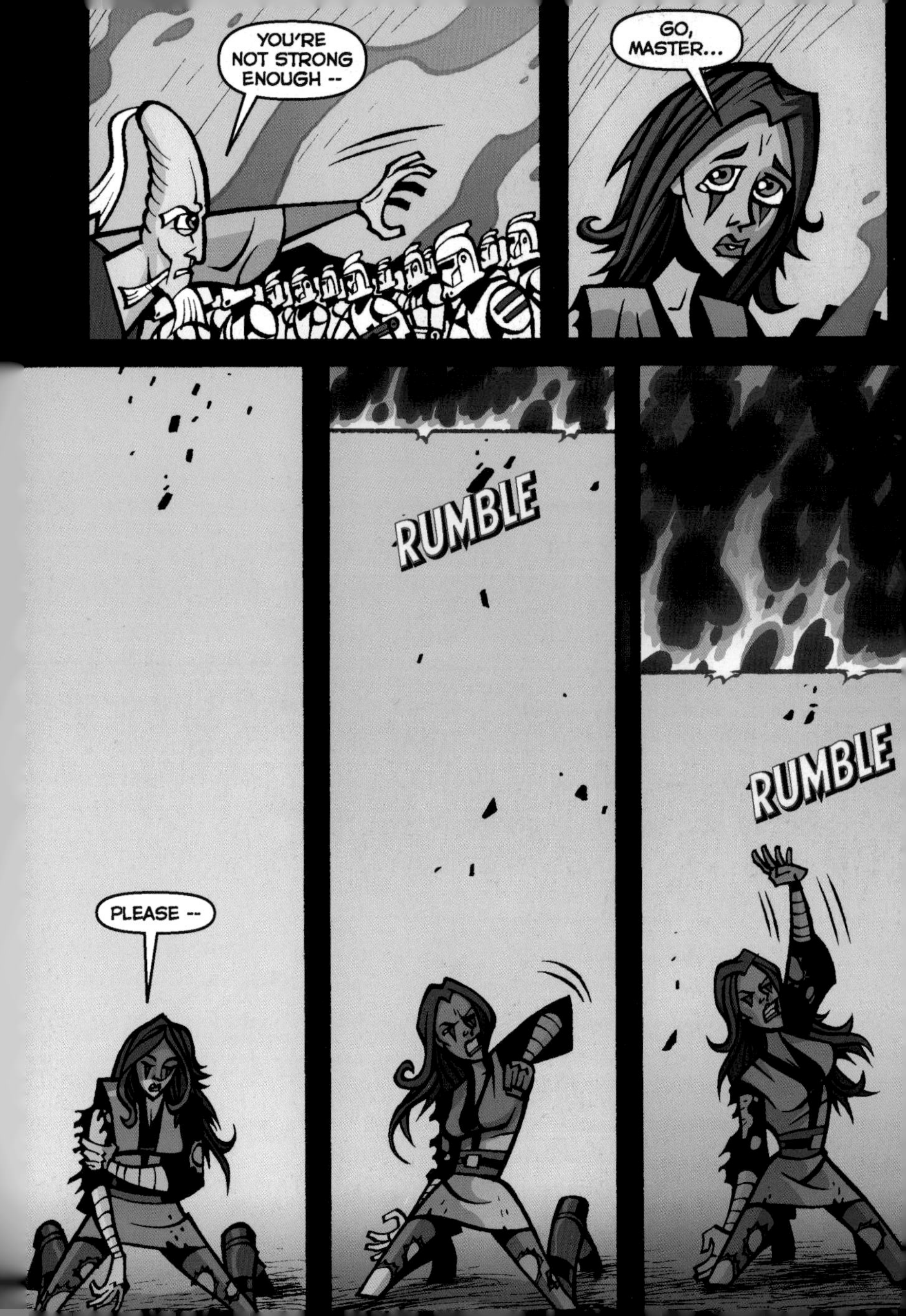
YOU'RE NOT STRONG ENOUGH --
GO, MASTER...
PLEASE --
RUMBLE
RUMBLE

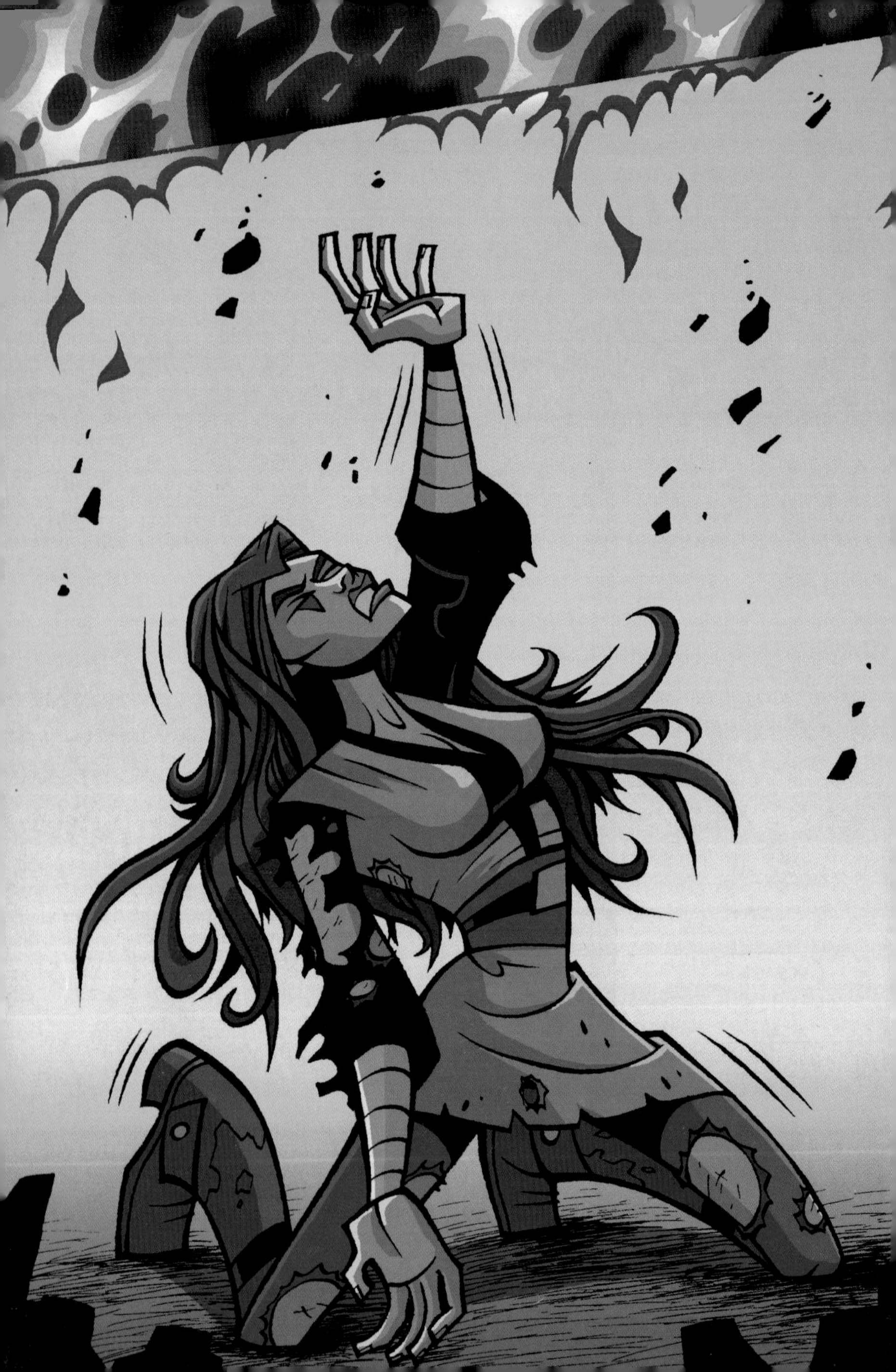

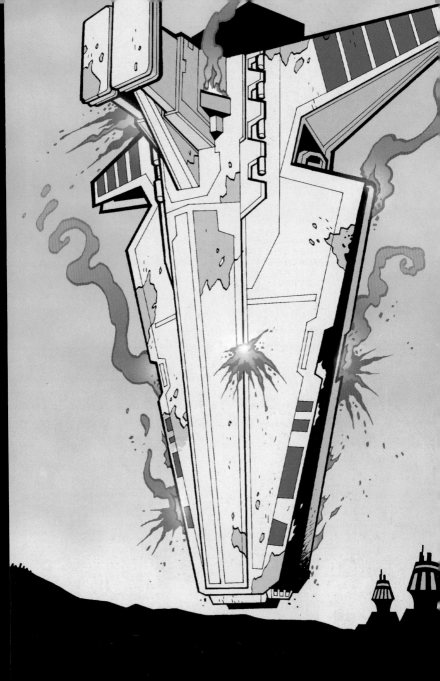

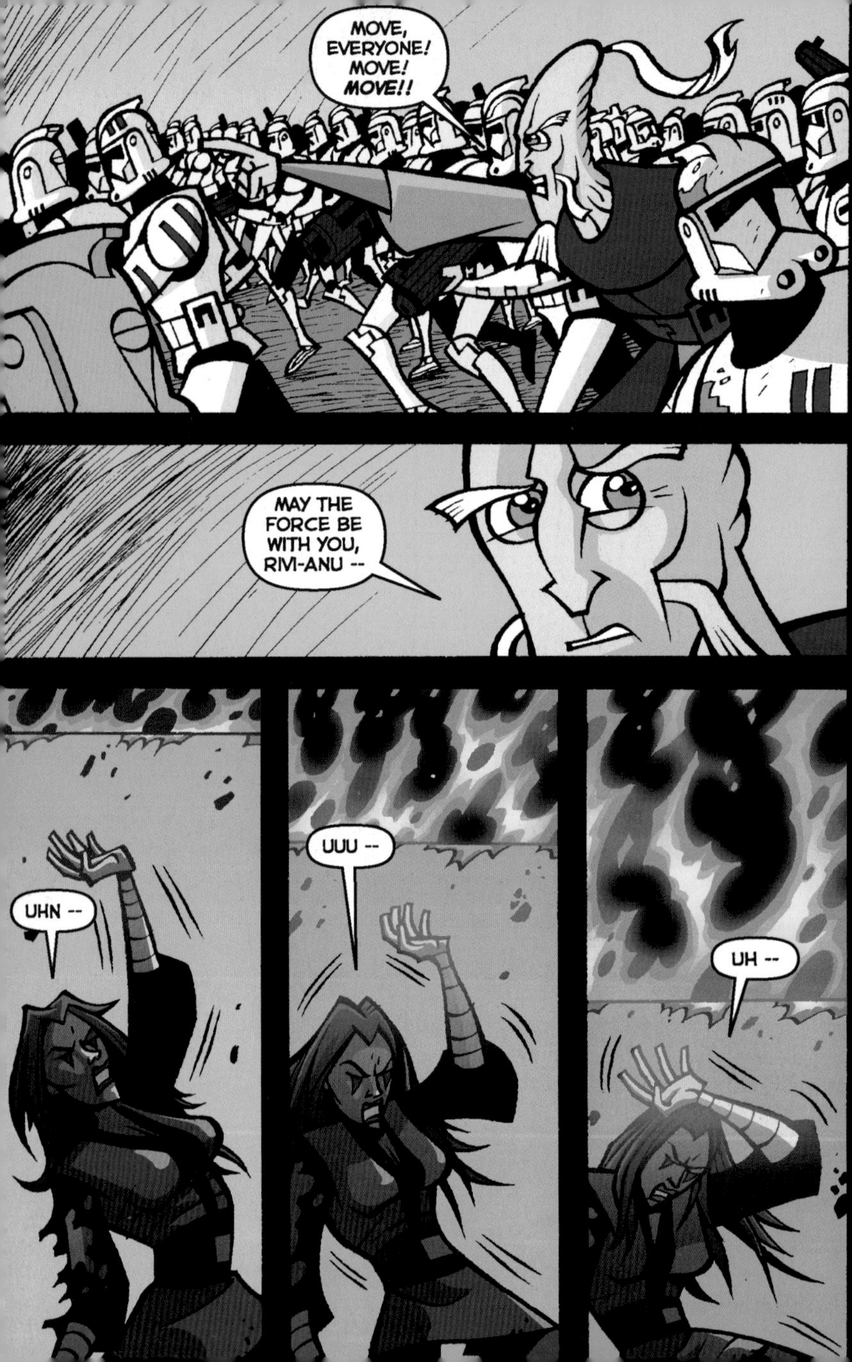
MOVE, EVERYONE! MOVE! *MOVE!!*
MAY THE FORCE BE WITH YOU, RIVI-ANU --
UHN --
UUU --
UH --

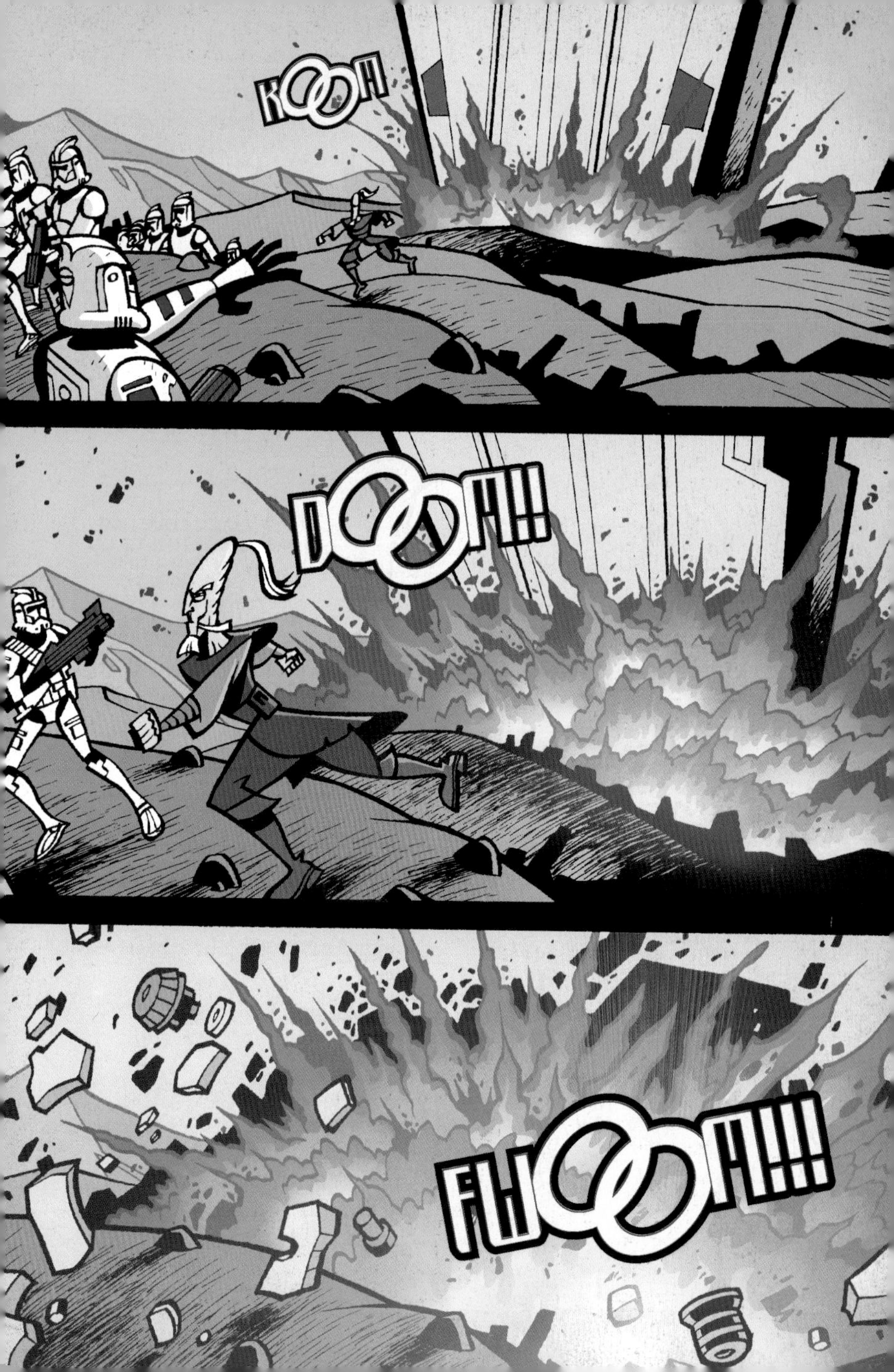
KOOM
DOOM!!
FWOOM!!!

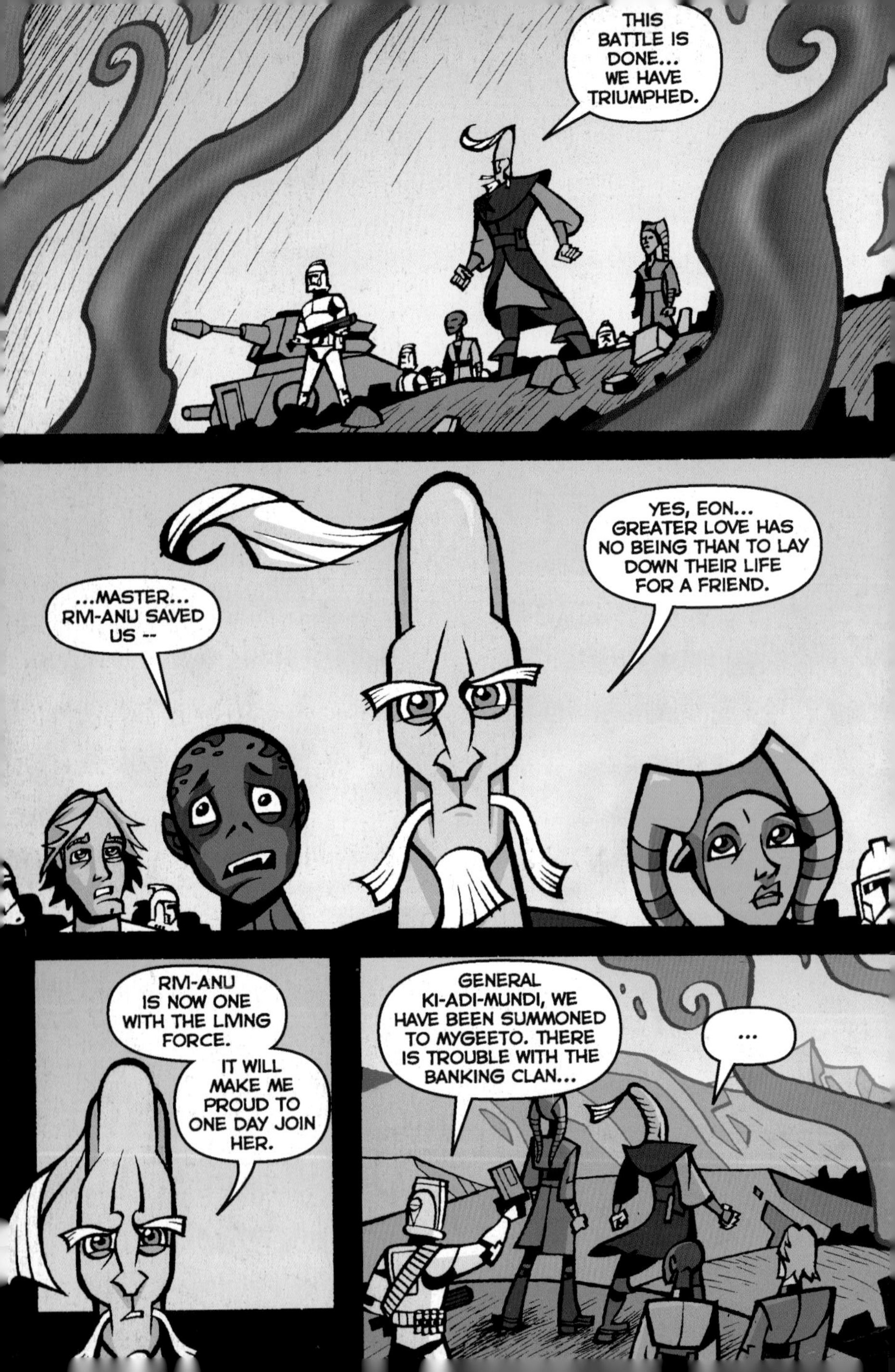
THIS BATTLE IS DONE... WE HAVE TRIUMPHED.
...MASTER... RIV-ANU SAVED US --
YES, EON... GREATER LOVE HAS NO BEING THAN TO LAY DOWN THEIR LIFE FOR A FRIEND.
RIV-ANU IS NOW ONE WITH THE LIVING FORCE.
IT WILL MAKE ME PROUD TO ONE DAY JOIN HER.
GENERAL KI-ADI-MUNDI, WE HAVE BEEN SUMMONED TO MYGEETO. THERE IS TROUBLE WITH THE BANKING CLAN...
...

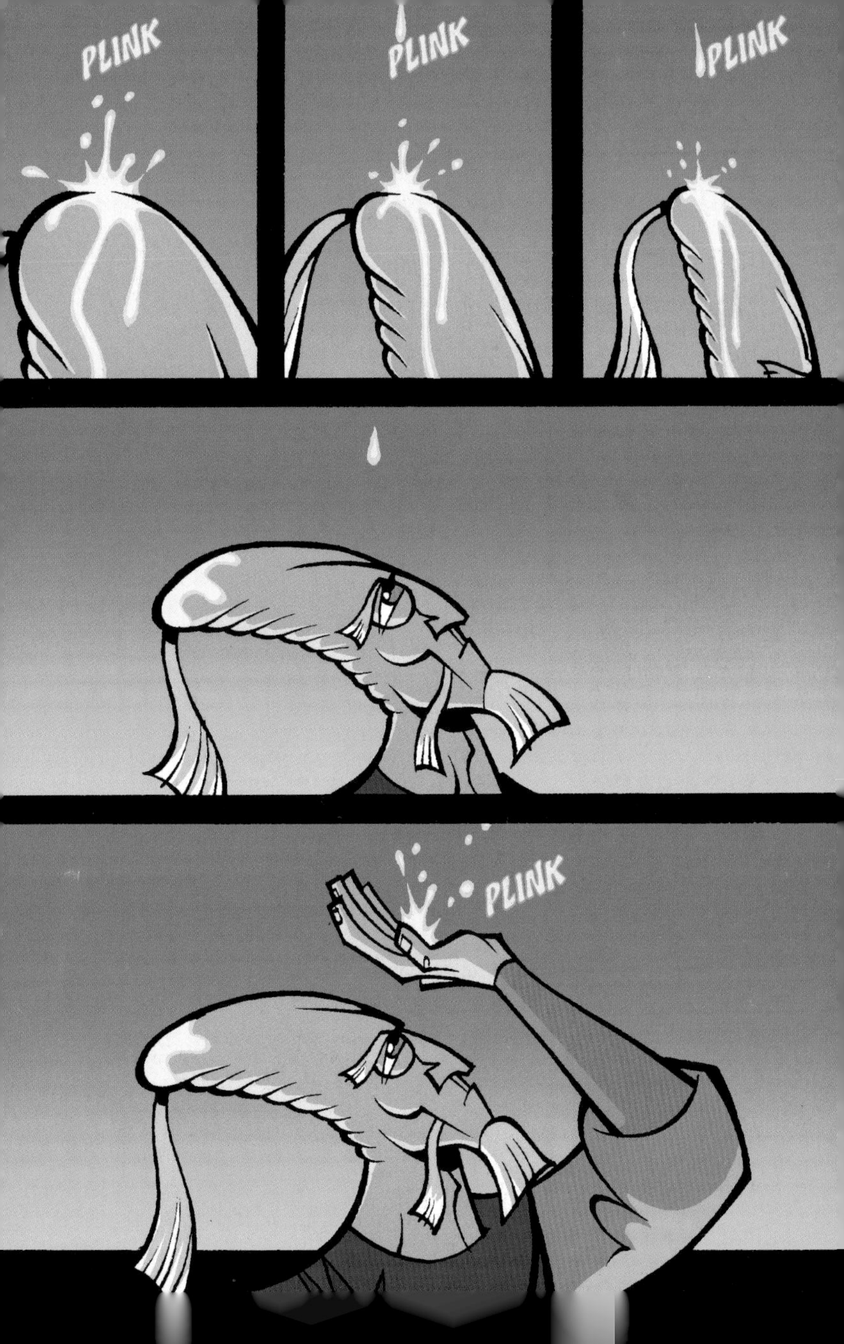
PLINK
PLINK
PLINK
PLINK

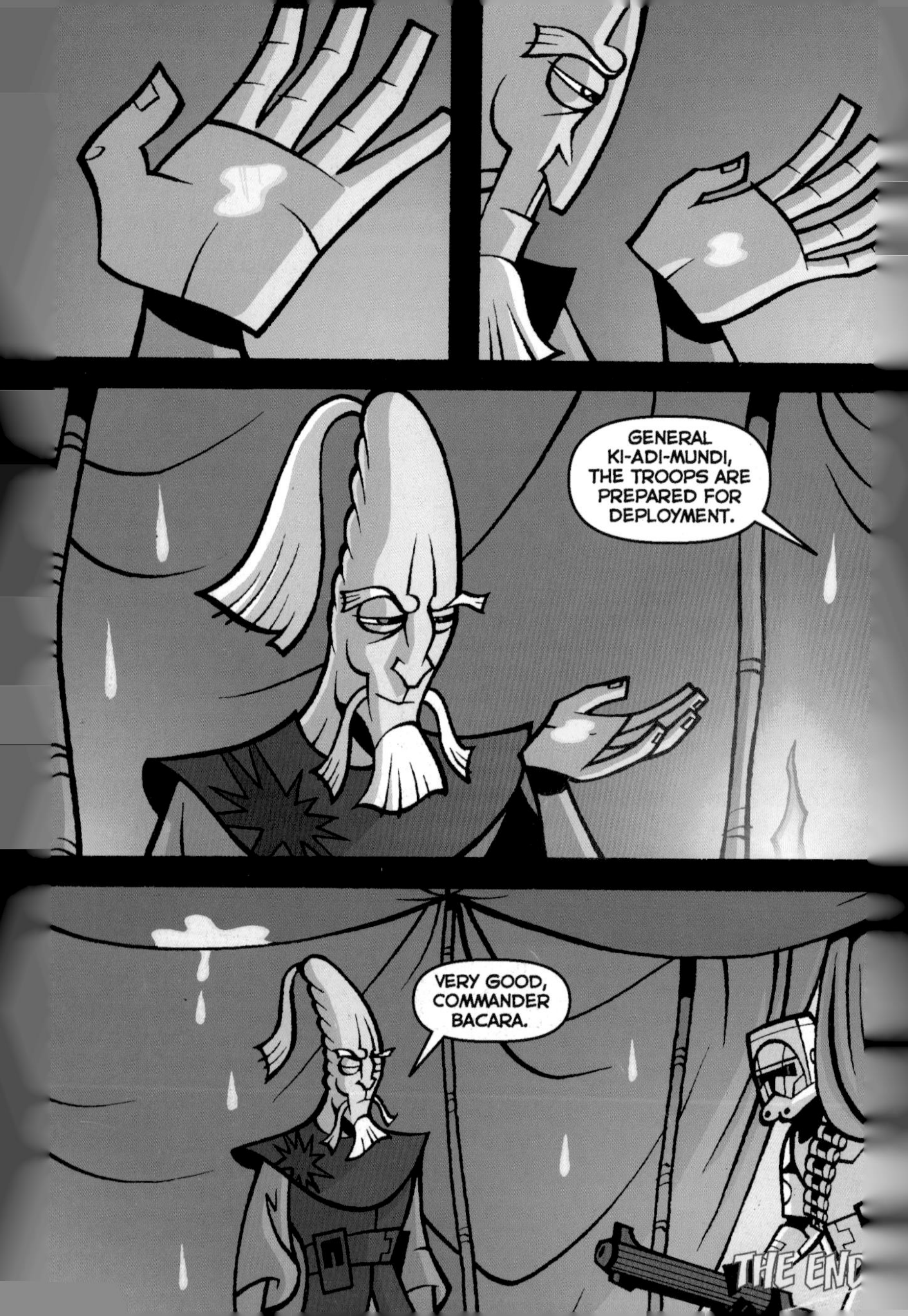
GENERAL KI-ADI-MUNDI, THE TROOPS ARE PREPARED FOR DEPLOYMENT.
VERY GOOD, COMMANDER BACARA.
THE END

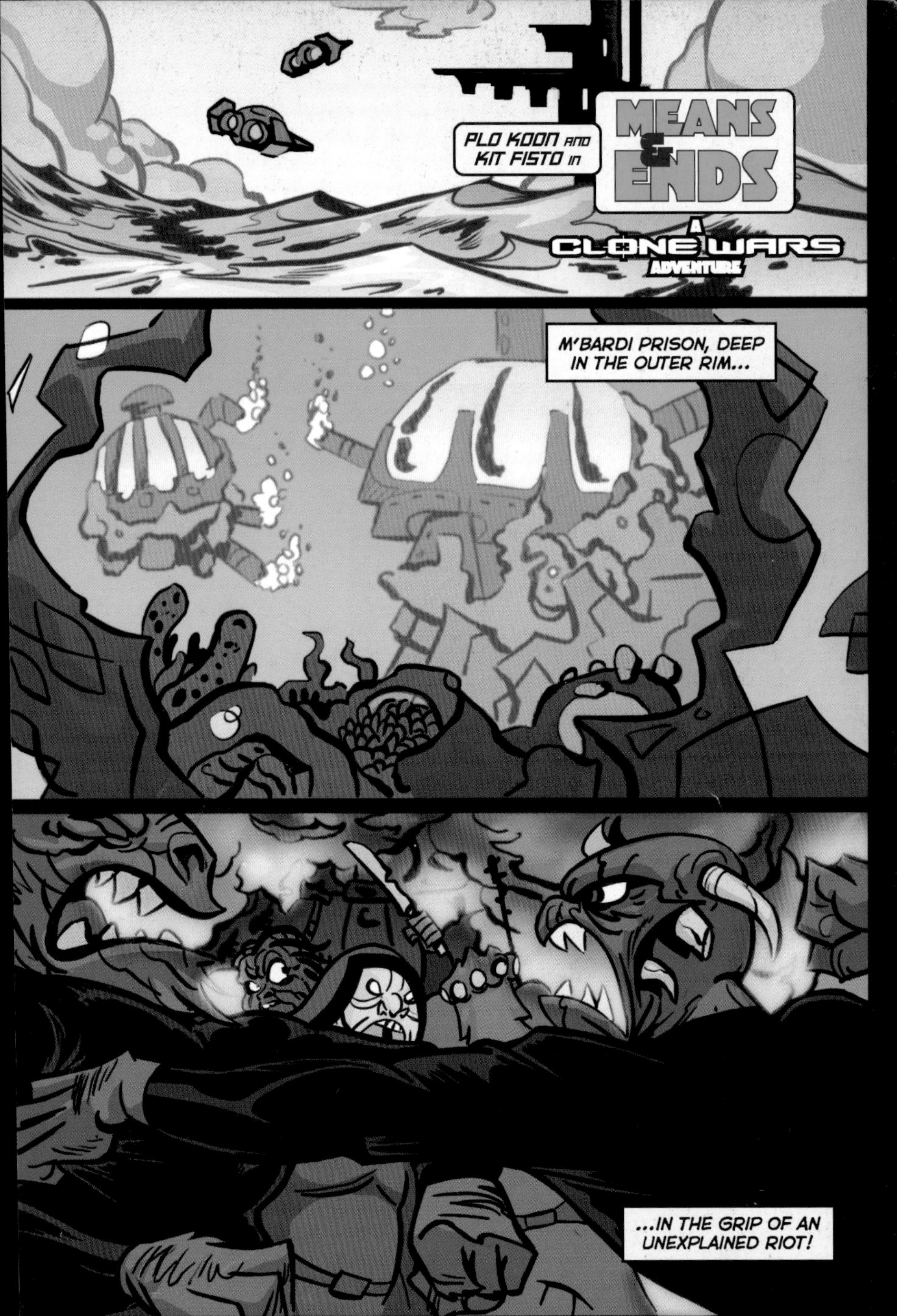
PLO KOON AND KIT FISTO IN
MEANS & ENDS
A CLONE WARS ADVENTURE
M'BARDI PRISON, DEEP IN THE OUTER RIM...
...IN THE GRIP OF AN UNEXPLAINED RIOT!

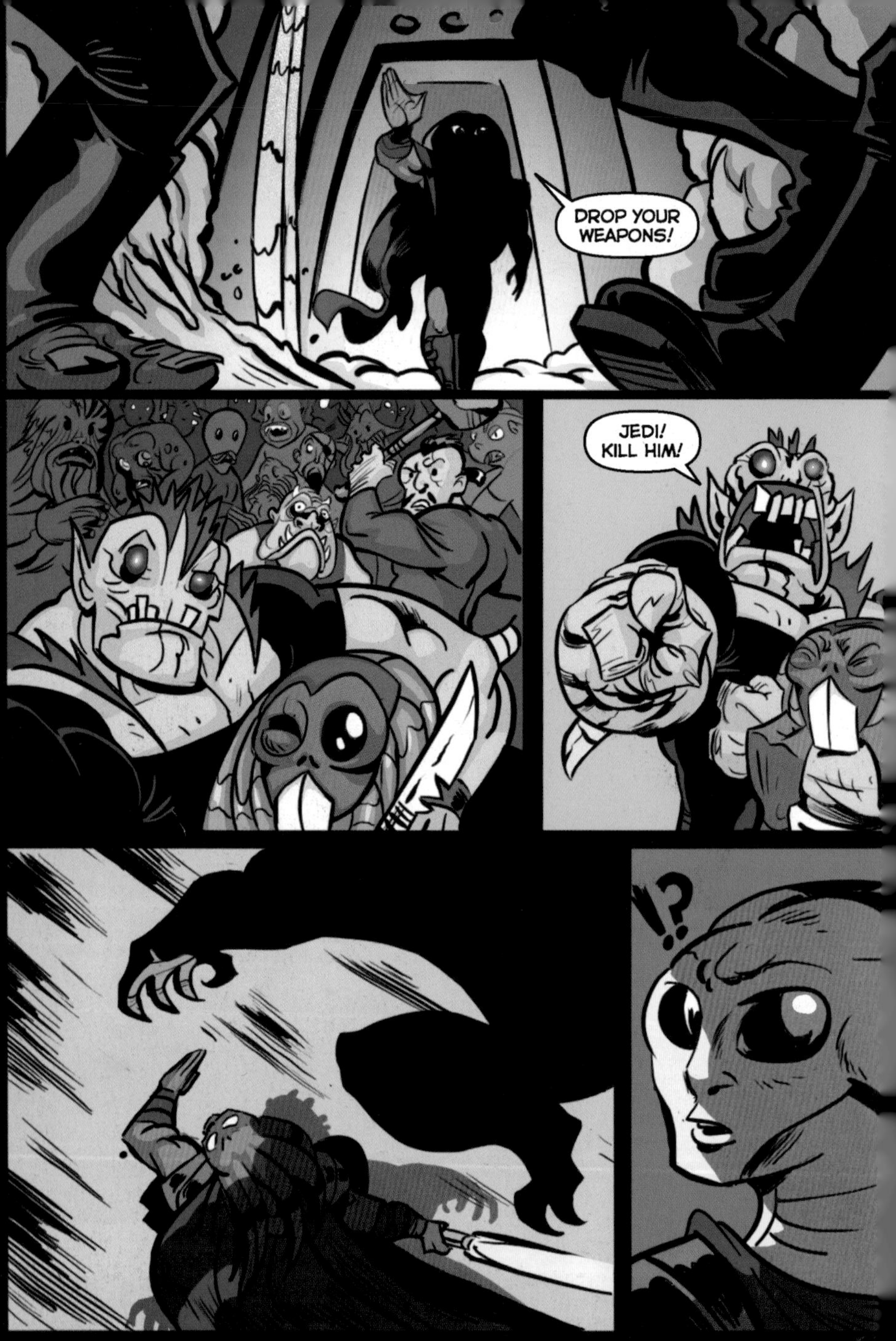
DROP YOUR WEAPONS!
JEDI! KILL HIM!
!?

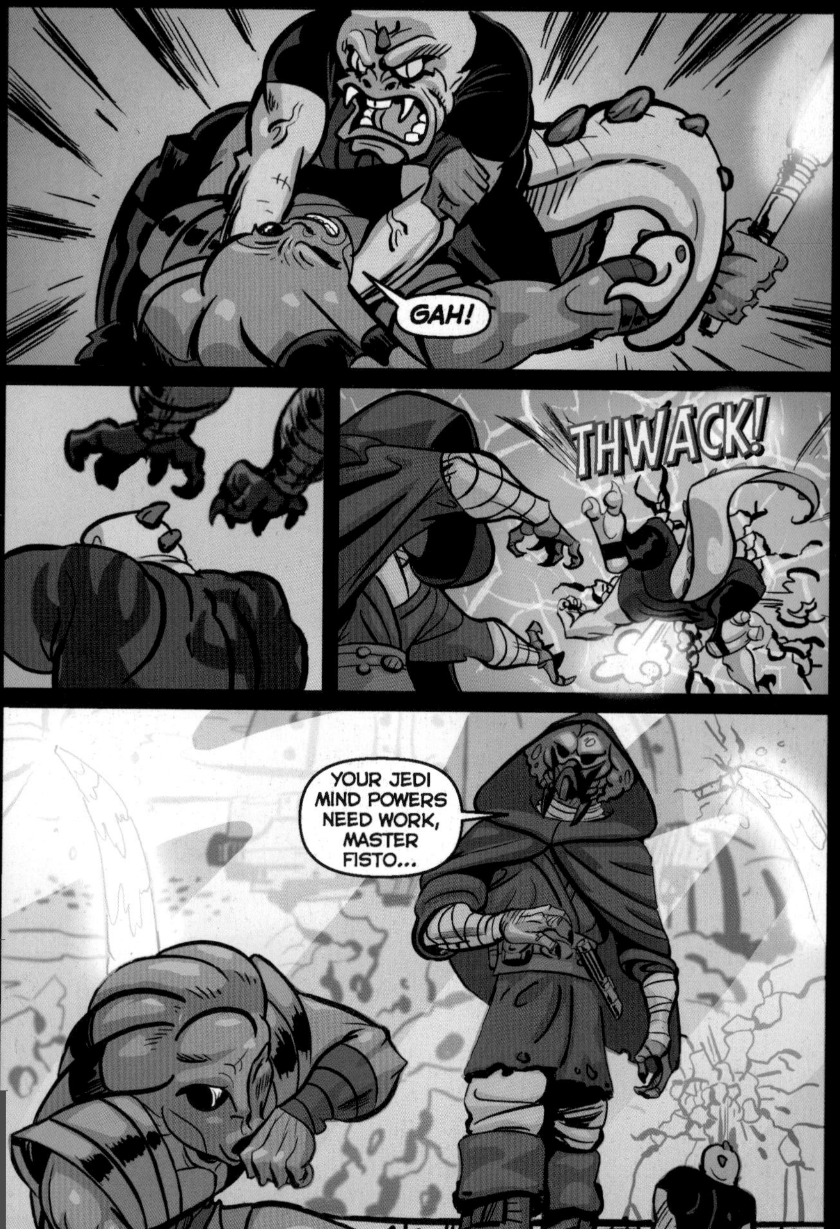
GAH!
THWACK!
YOUR JEDI MIND POWERS NEED WORK, MASTER FISTO...

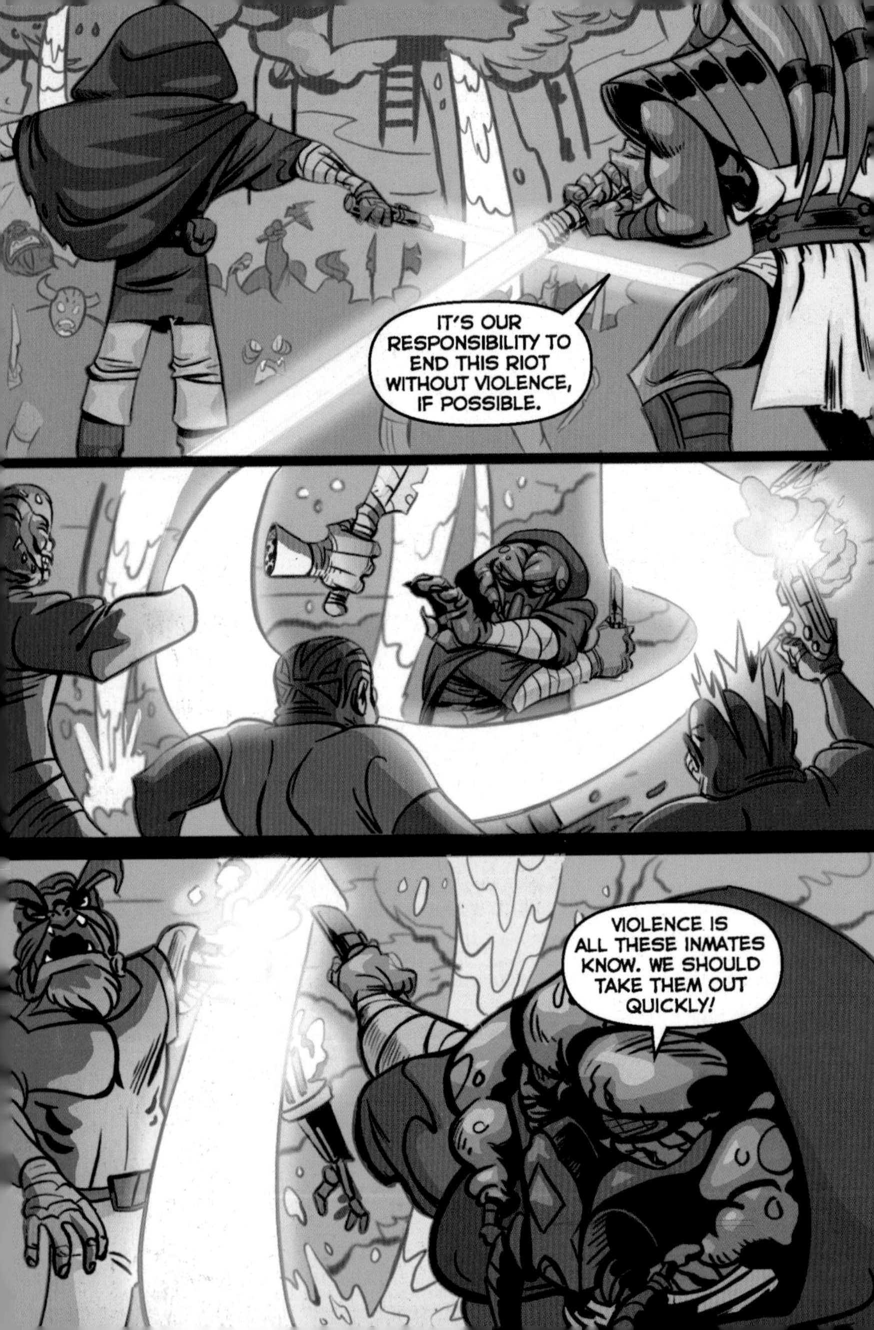
IT'S OUR RESPONSIBILITY TO END THIS RIOT WITHOUT VIOLENCE, IF POSSIBLE.
VIOLENCE IS ALL THESE INMATES KNOW. WE SHOULD TAKE THEM OUT QUICKLY!

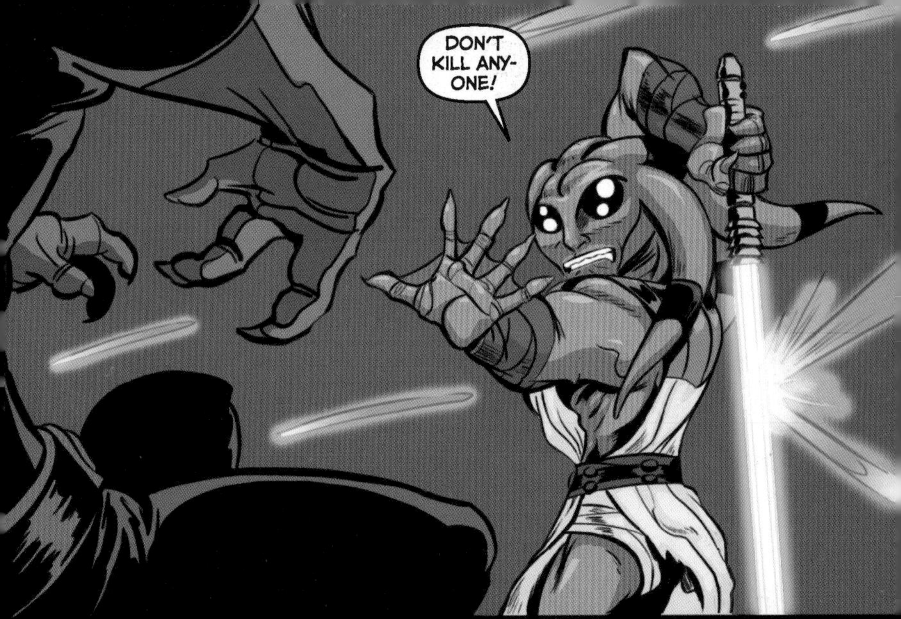
DON'T KILL ANY-ONE!

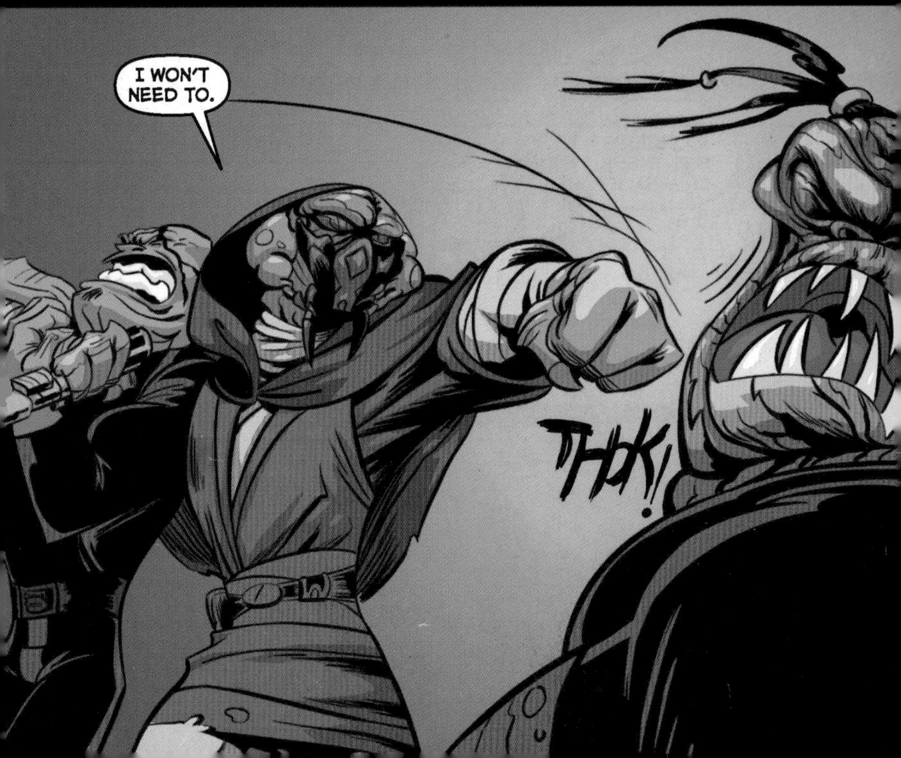
I WON'T NEED TO.
THOK!

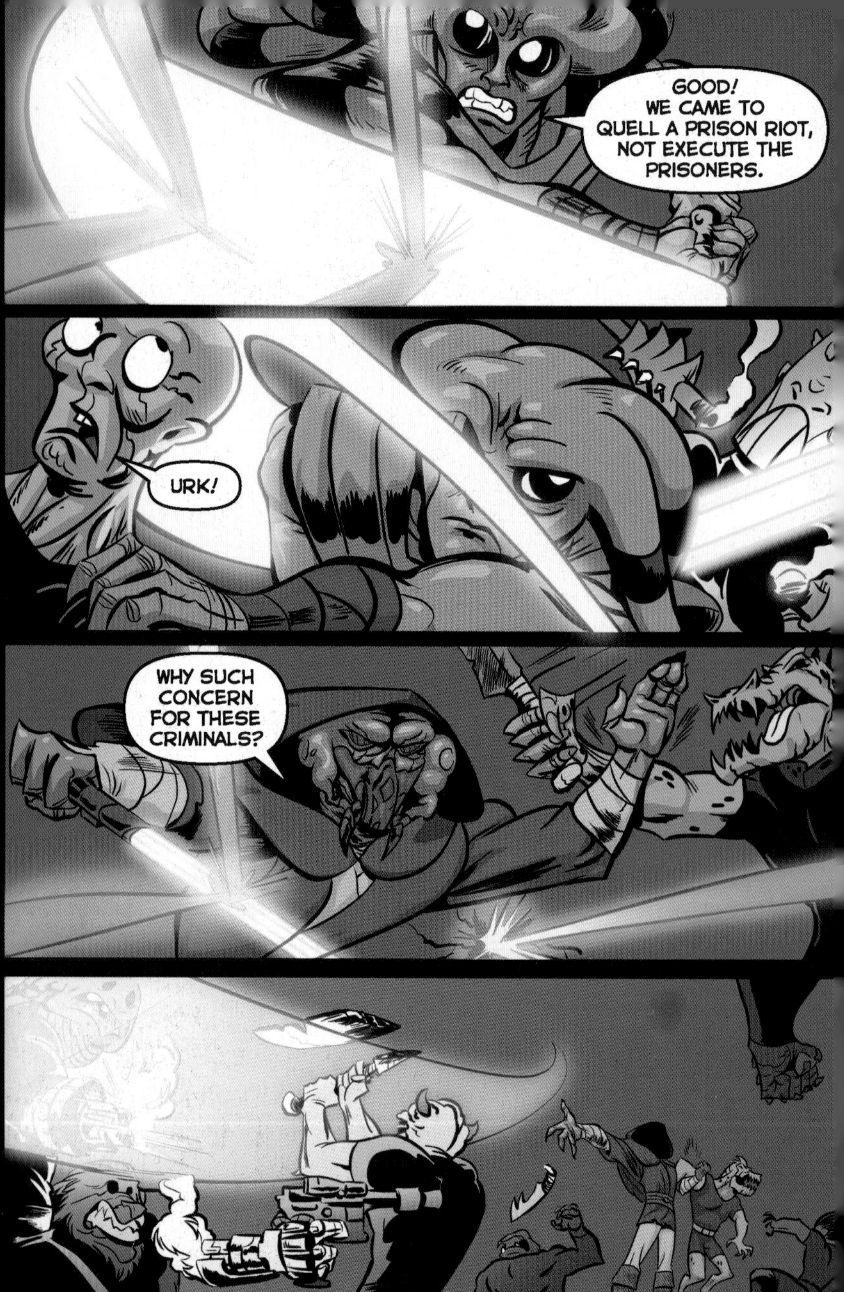
GOOD! WE CAME TO QUELL A PRISON RIOT, NOT EXECUTE THE PRISONERS.
URK!
WHY SUCH CONCERN FOR THESE CRIMINALS?

I JUST BELIEVE IN SECOND CHANCES.

SCUM LIKE THIS CAN'T BE REHABILI-TATED.

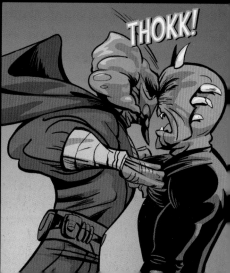

THOKK!

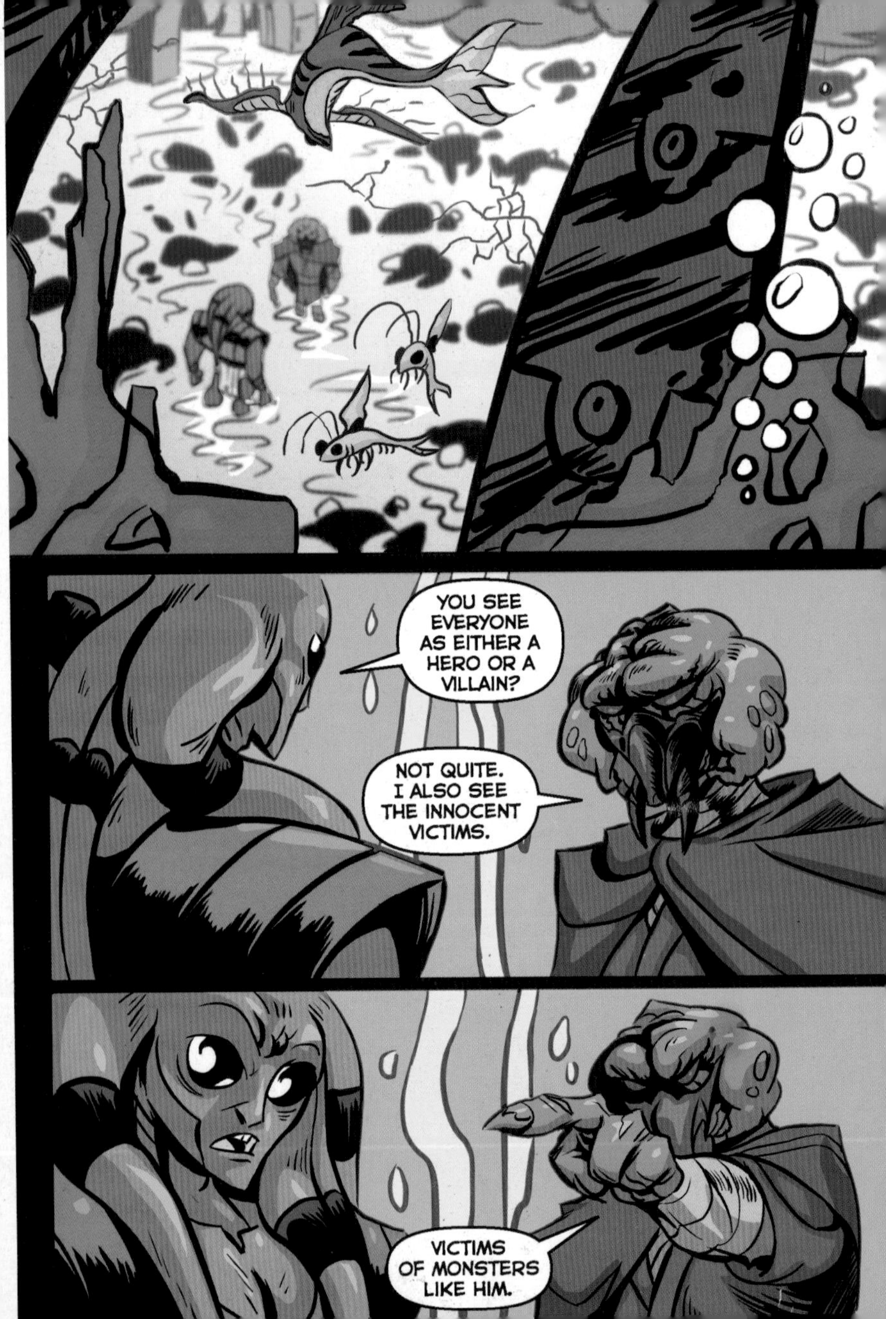
YOU SEE EVERYONE AS EITHER A HERO OR A VILLAIN?
NOT QUITE. I ALSO SEE THE INNOCENT VICTIMS.
VICTIMS OF MONSTERS LIKE HIM.

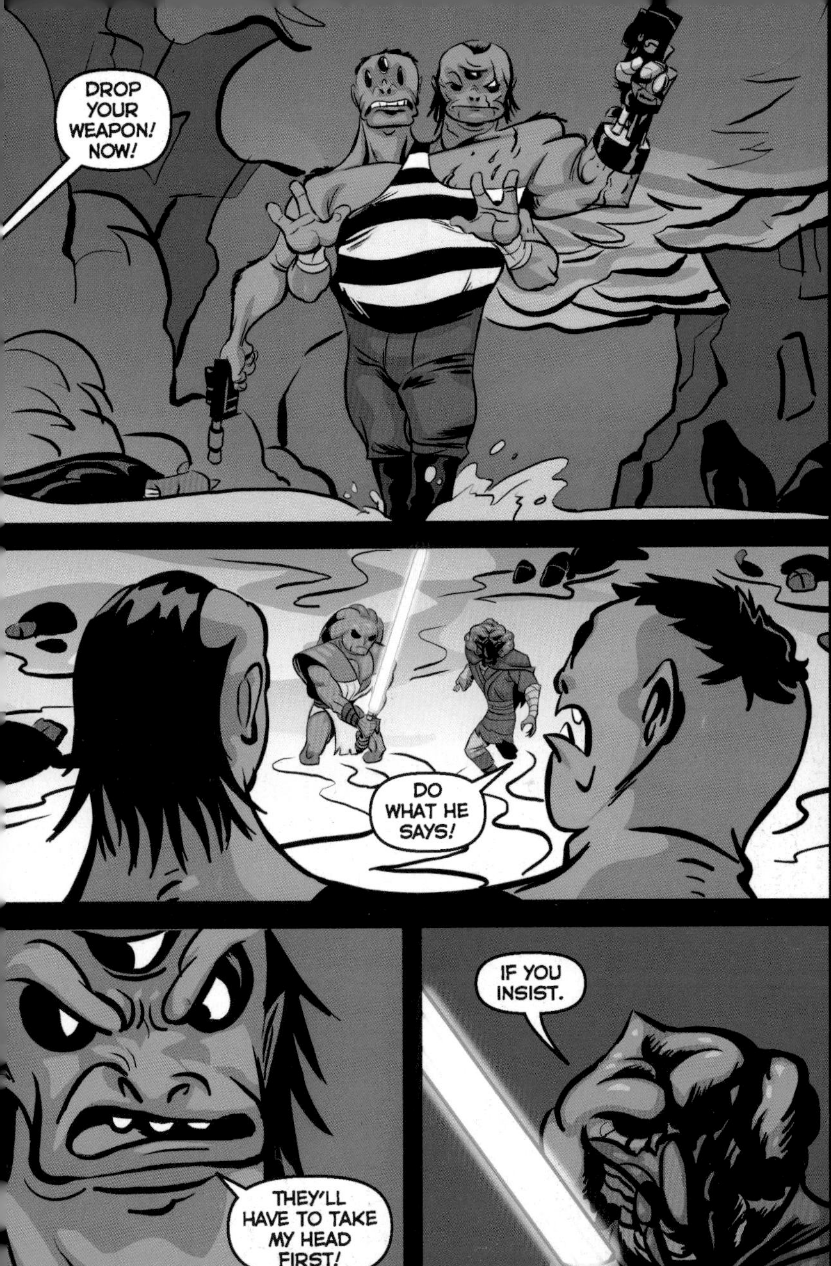
DROP YOUR WEAPON! NOW!
DO WHAT HE SAYS!
THEY'LL HAVE TO TAKE MY HEAD FIRST!
IF YOU INSIST.

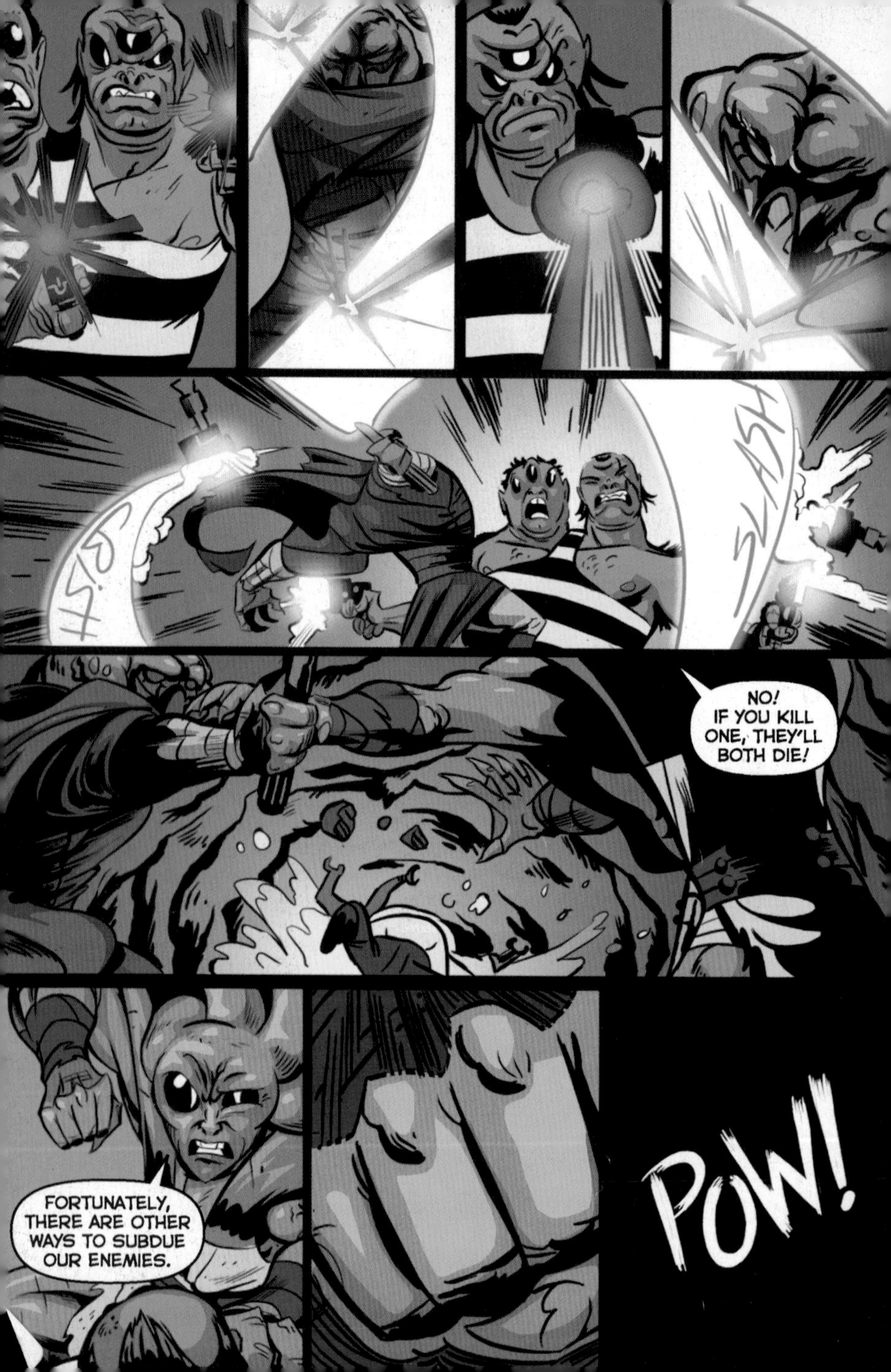
SLASH
NO! IF YOU KILL ONE, THEY'LL BOTH DIE!
FORTUNATELY, THERE ARE OTHER WAYS TO SUBDUE OUR ENEMIES.
POW!

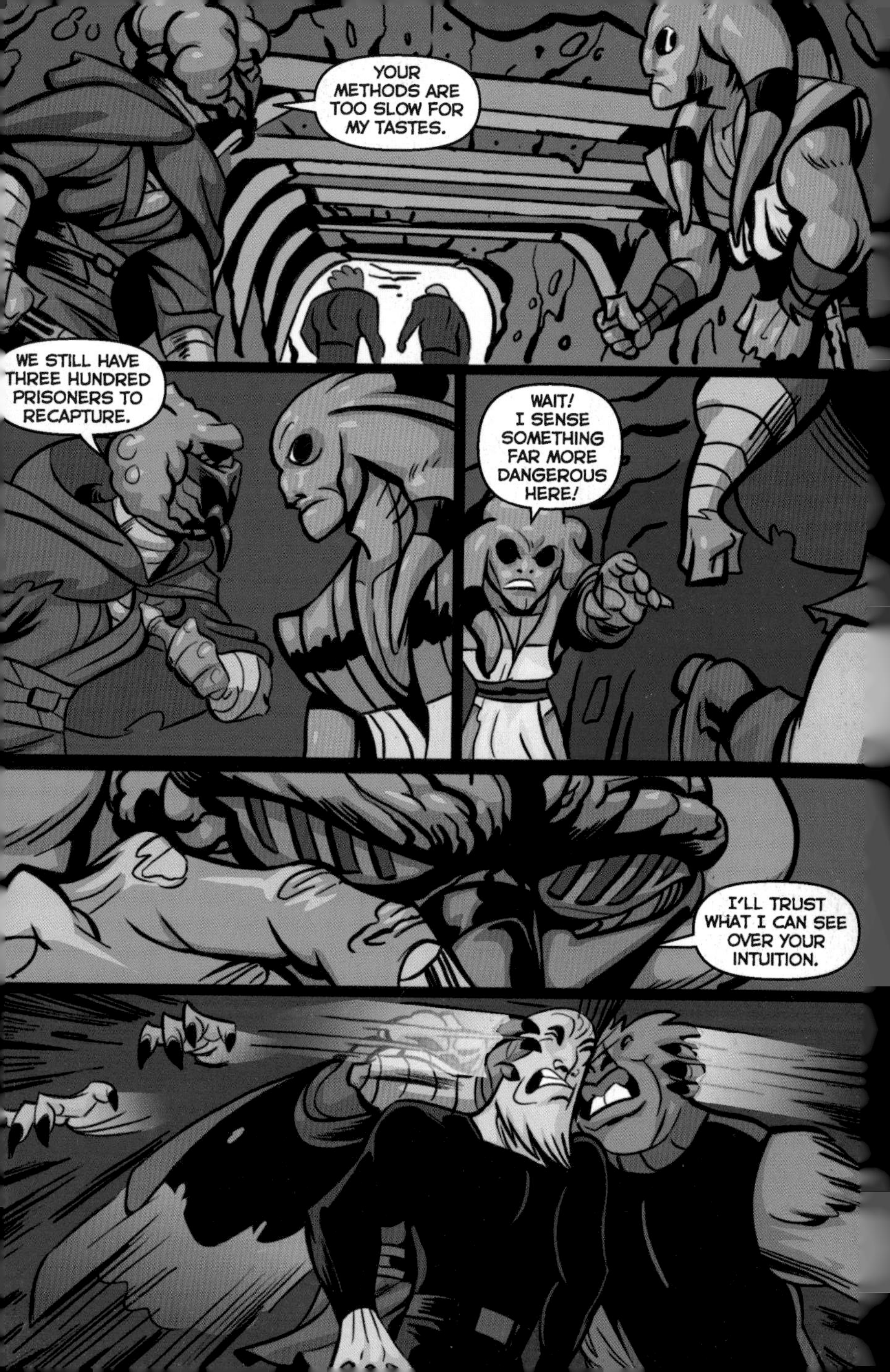
YOUR METHODS ARE TOO SLOW FOR MY TASTES.
WE STILL HAVE THREE HUNDRED PRISONERS TO RECAPTURE.
WAIT! I SENSE SOMETHING FAR MORE DANGEROUS HERE!
I'LL TRUST WHAT I CAN SEE OVER YOUR INTUITION.

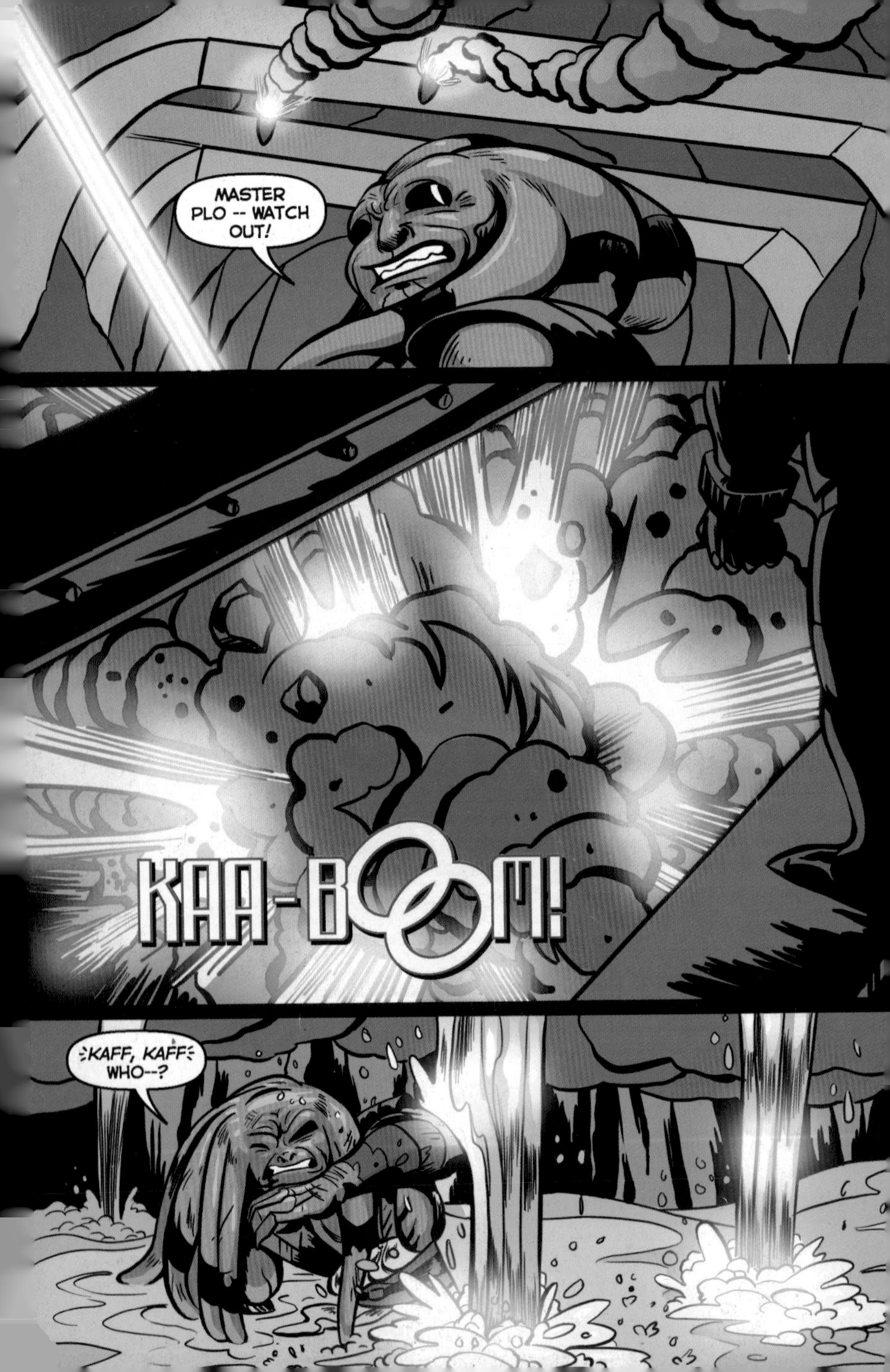
MASTER PLO -- WATCH OUT!
KAA-BOOM!
KAFF, KAFF WHO--?

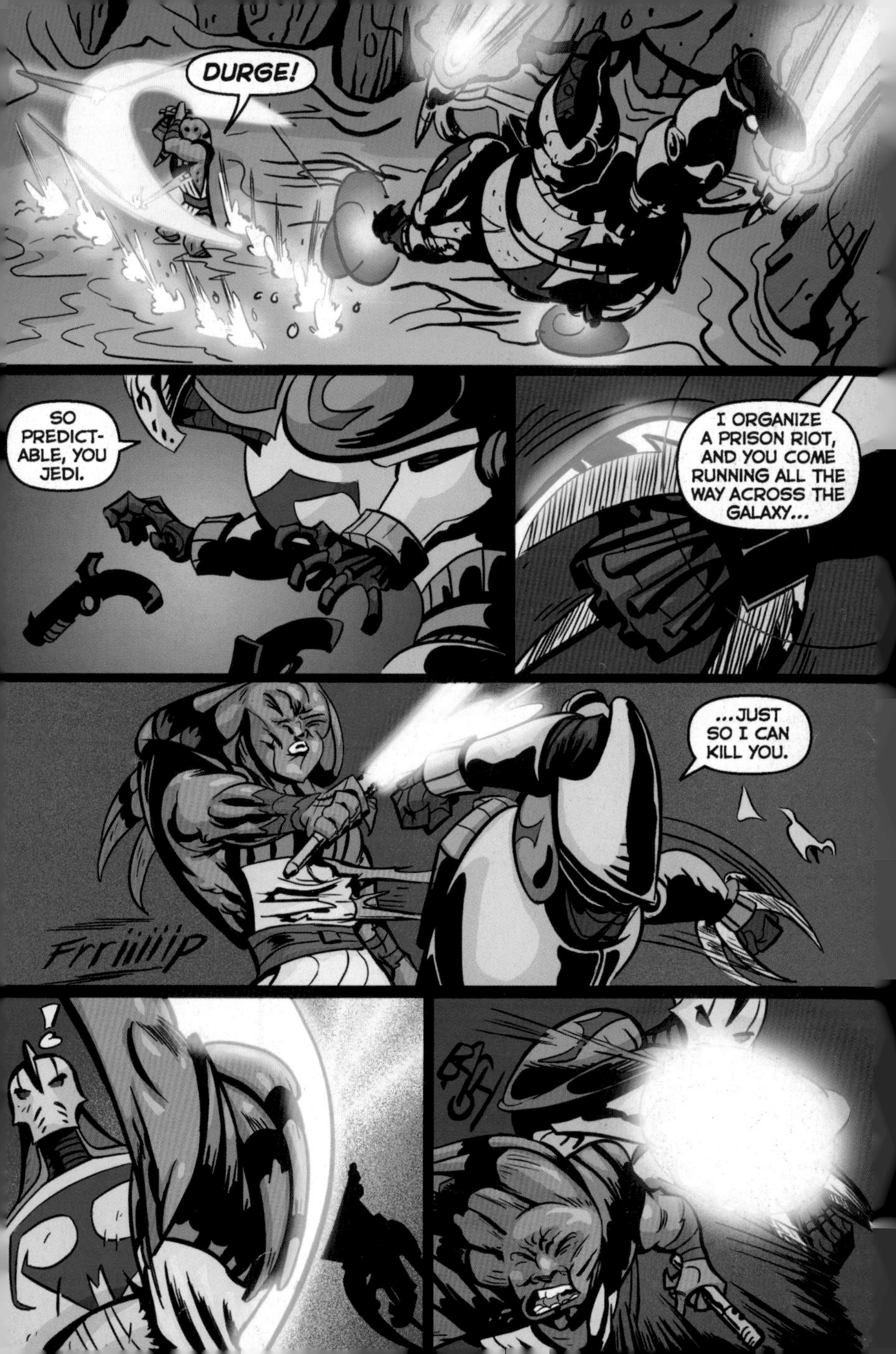
DURGE!
SO PREDICT-ABLE, YOU JEDI.
I ORGANIZE A PRISON RIOT, AND YOU COME RUNNING ALL THE WAY ACROSS THE GALAXY...
...JUST SO I CAN KILL YOU.
Frriiiiip
!

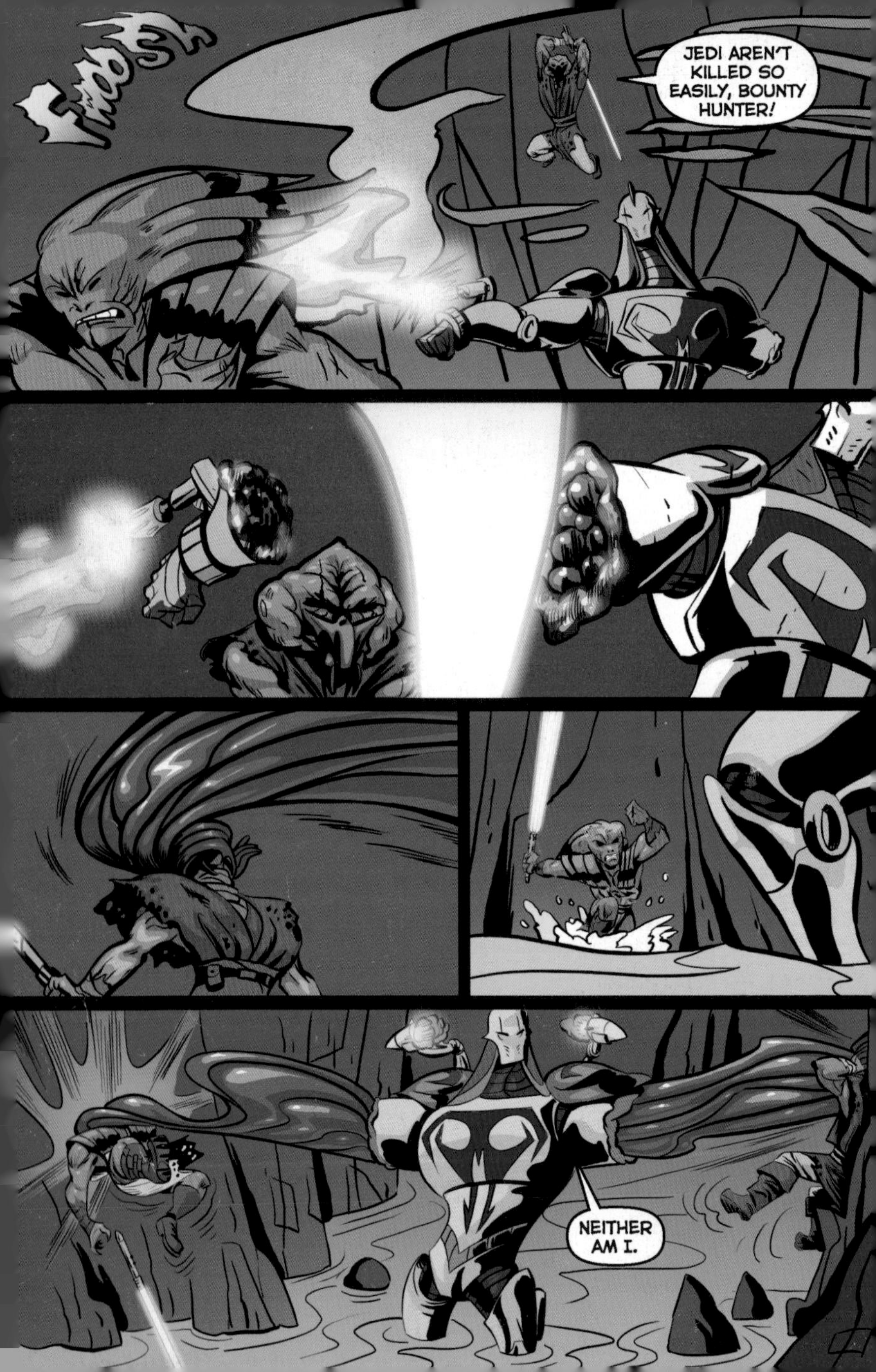
FWOOSH
JEDI AREN'T KILLED SO EASILY, BOUNTY HUNTER!
NEITHER AM I.

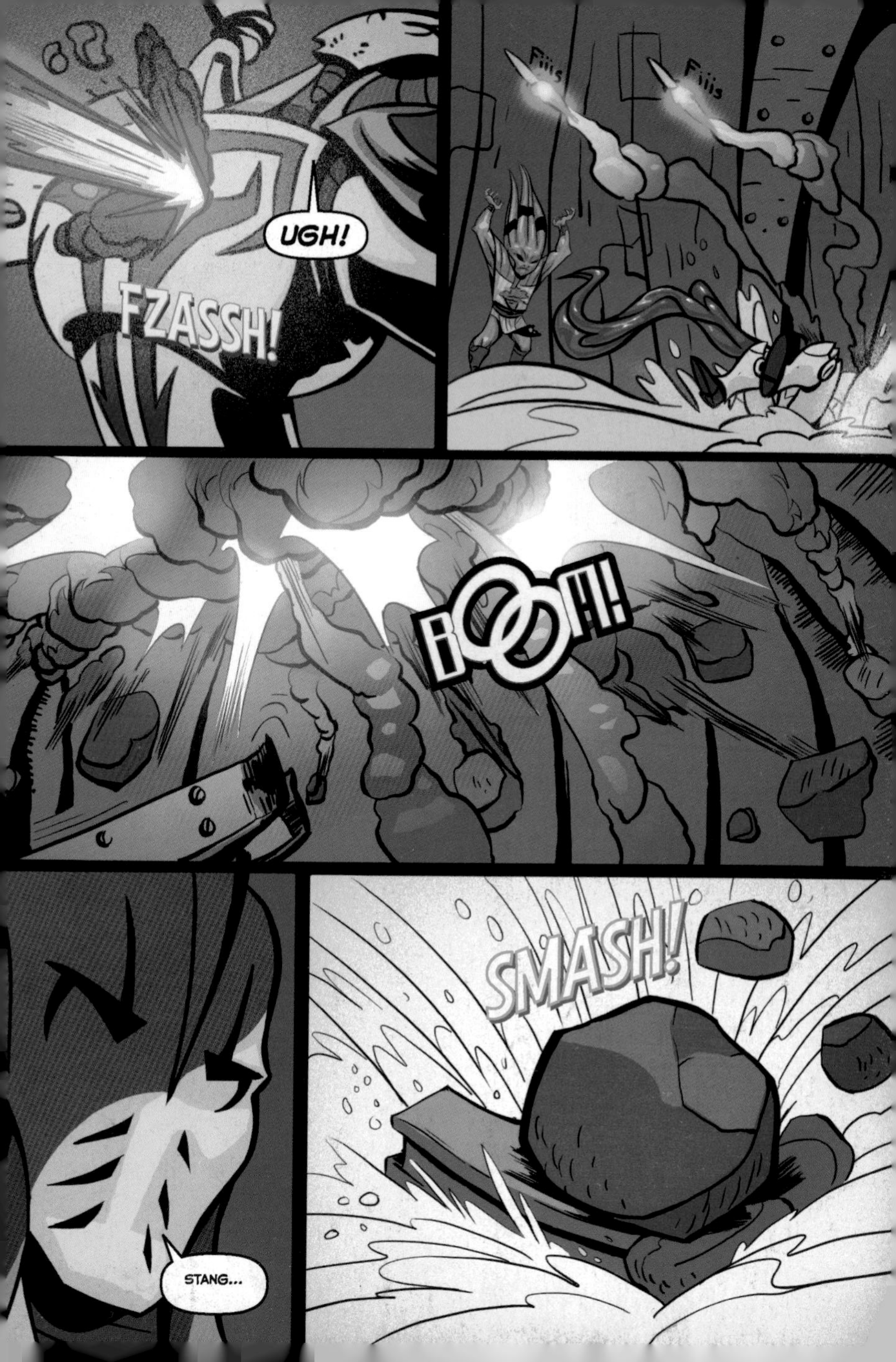
UGH!
FZASSH!
Fiiis
Fiiis
BOOM!
SMASH!
STANG...

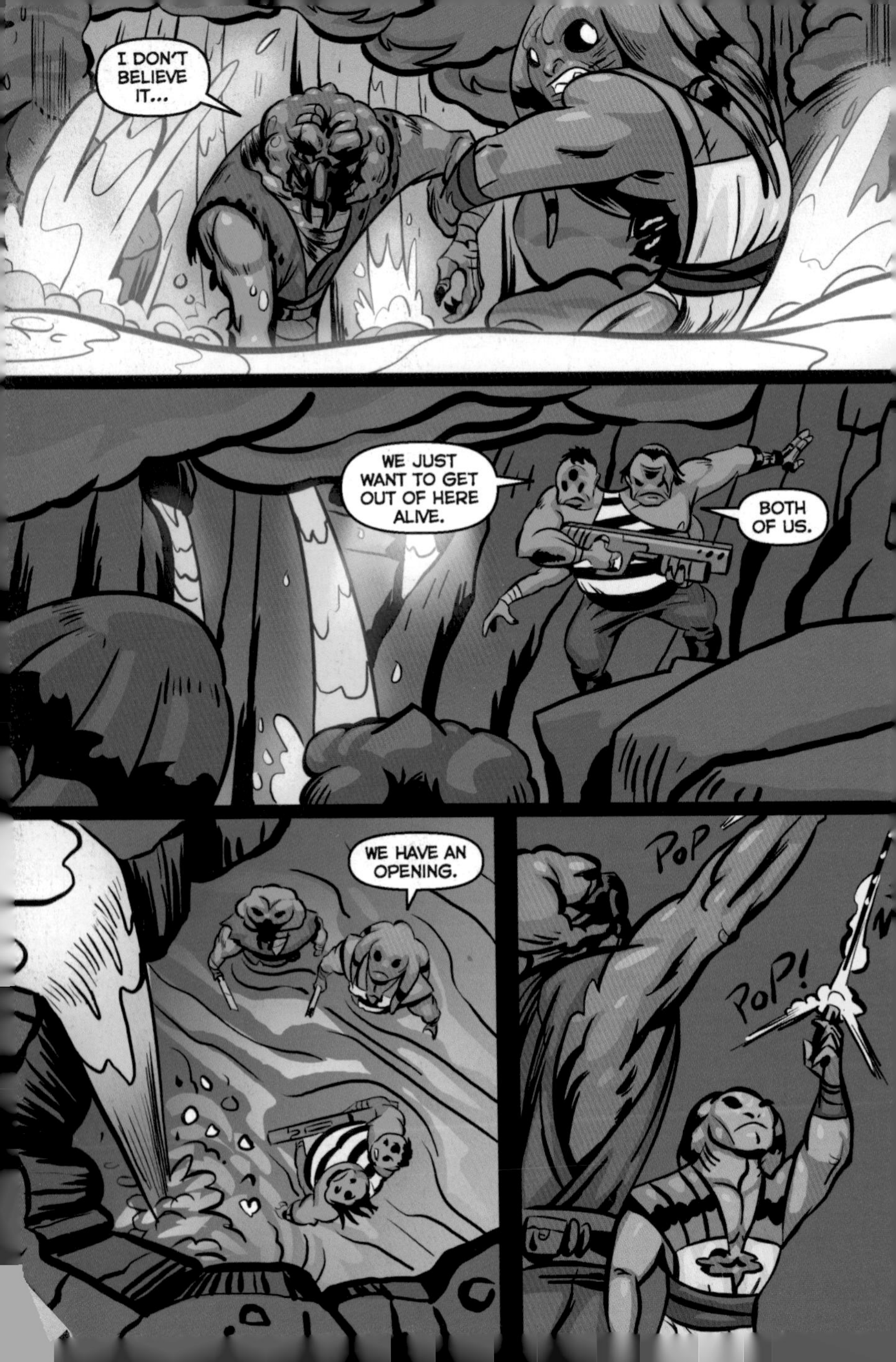
I DON'T BELIEVE IT...
WE JUST WANT TO GET OUT OF HERE ALIVE.
BOTH OF US.
WE HAVE AN OPENING.
POP
POP!

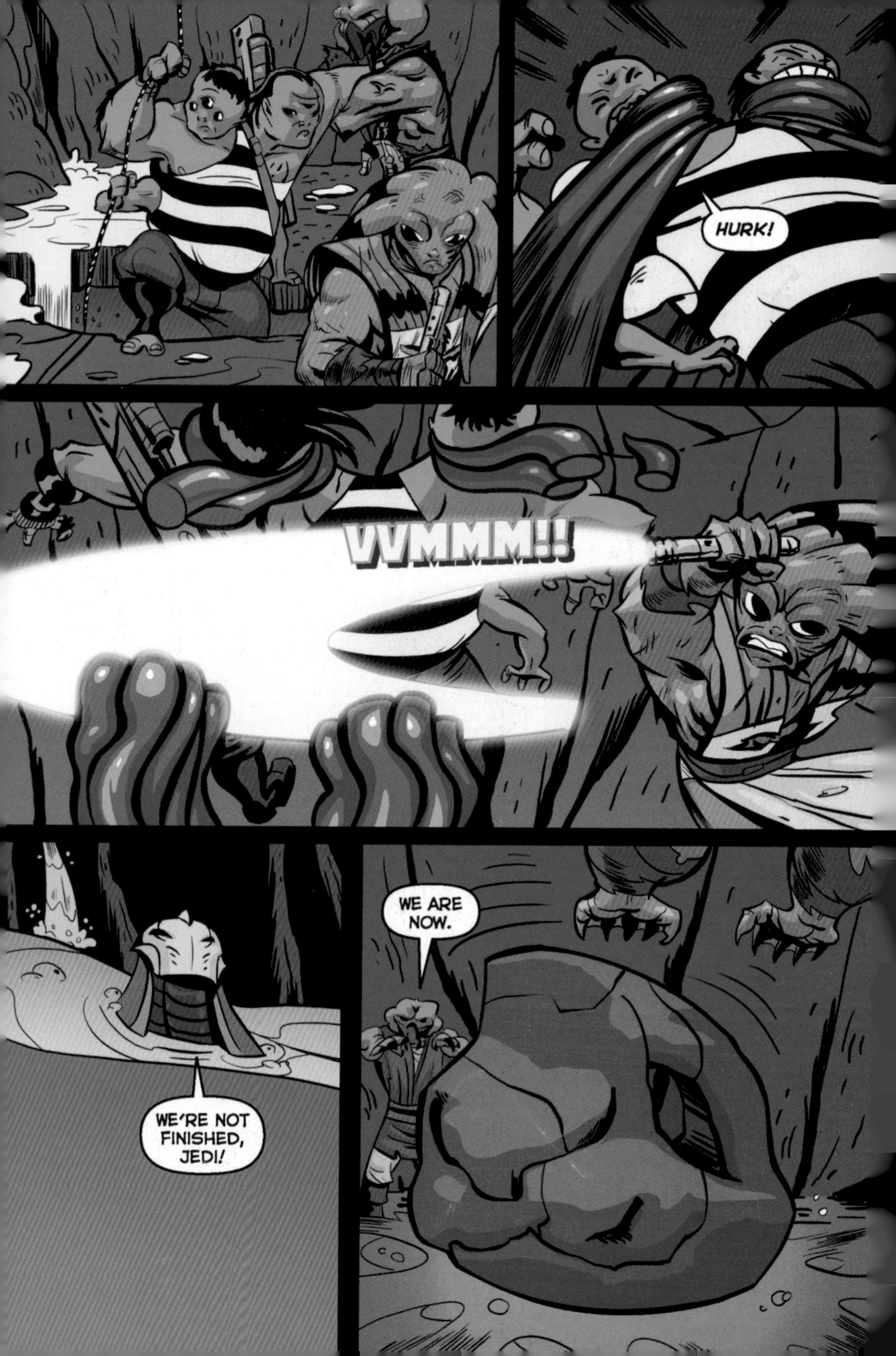
HURK!
VVMMMM!!
WE'RE NOT FINISHED, JEDI!
WE ARE NOW.

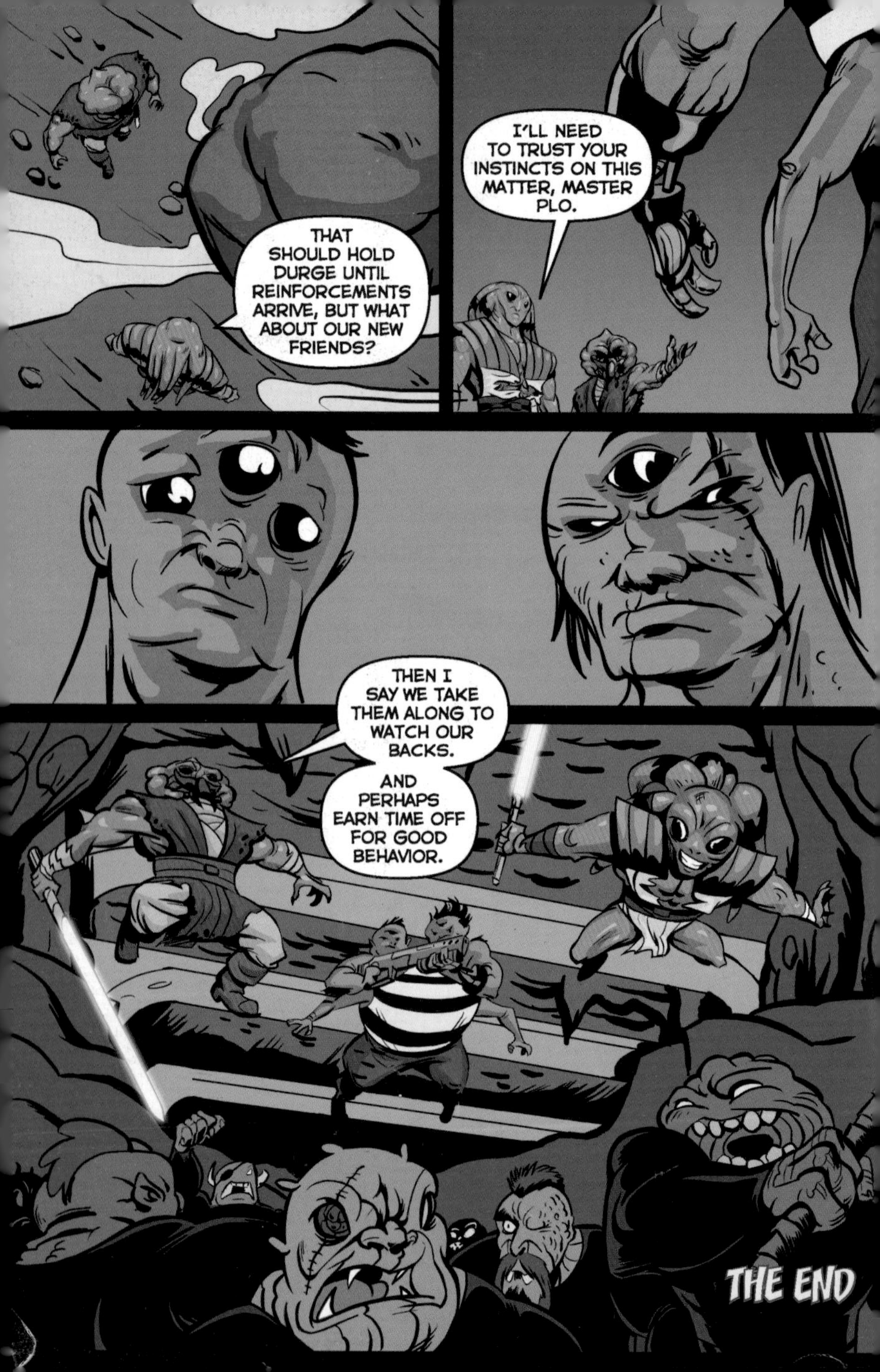
THAT SHOULD HOLD DURGE UNTIL REINFORCEMENTS ARRIVE, BUT WHAT ABOUT OUR NEW FRIENDS?
I'LL NEED TO TRUST YOUR INSTINCTS ON THIS MATTER, MASTER PLO.
THEN I SAY WE TAKE THEM ALONG TO WATCH OUR BACKS.
AND PERHAPS EARN TIME OFF FOR GOOD BEHAVIOR.
THE END

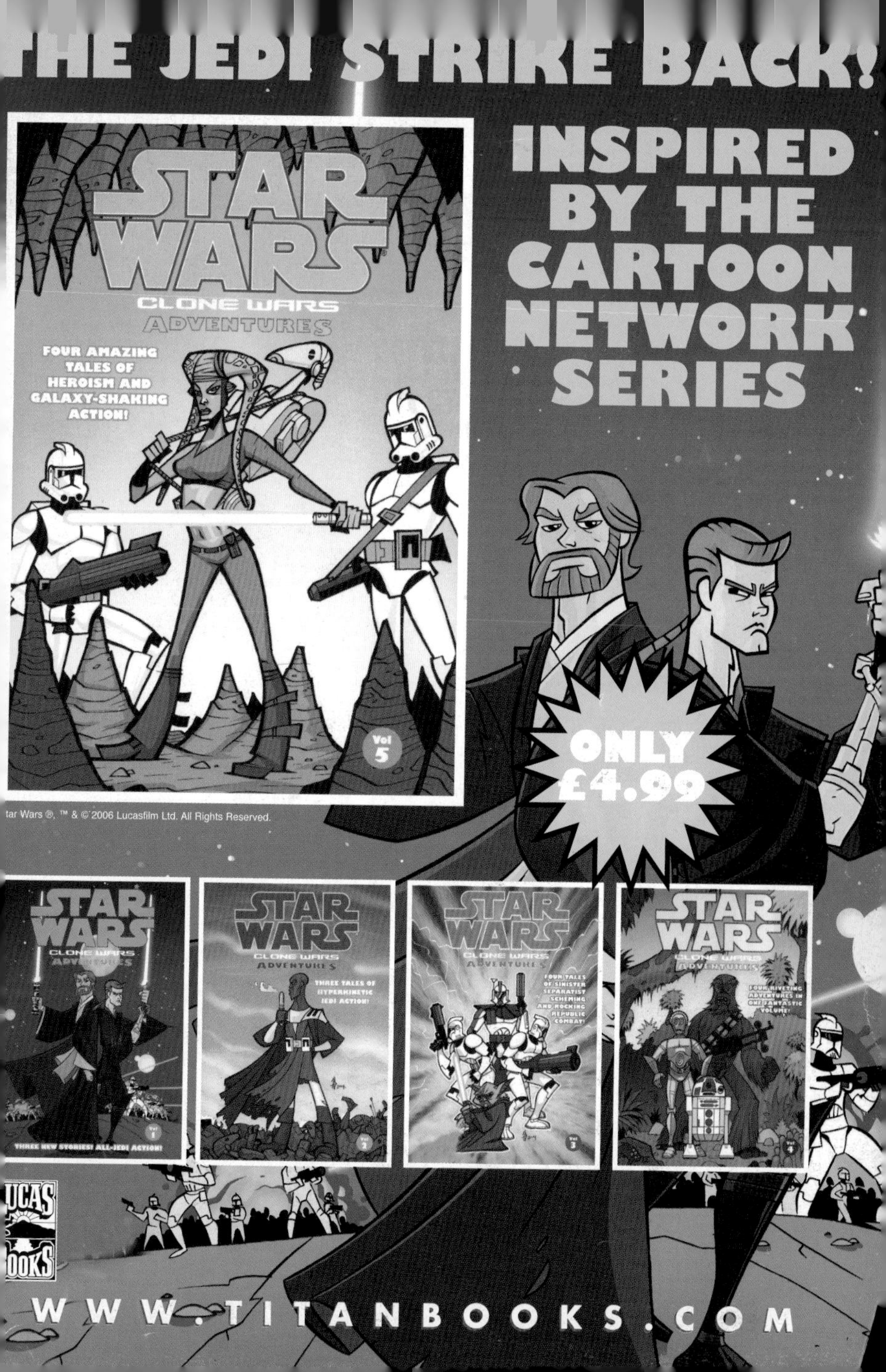
THE JEDI STRIKE BACK!
STAR WARS
CLONE WARS
ADVENTURES
FOUR AMAZING TALES OF HEROISM AND GALAXY-SHAKING ACTION!
Vol 5
INSPIRED BY THE CARTOON NETWORK SERIES
ONLY £4.99
tar Wars ®, ™ & © 2006 Lucasfilm Ltd. All Rights Reserved.
STAR WARS CLONE WARS ADVENTURES
THREE NEW STORIES! ALL-JEDI ACTION!
STAR WARS CLONE WARS ADVENTURES
THREE TALES OF HYPERKINETIC JEDI ACTION!
STAR WARS CLONE WARS ADVENTURES
FOUR TALES OF SINISTER SEPARATIST SCHEMING AND ROCKING REPUBLIC COMBAT!
STAR WARS CLONE WARS ADVENTURES
FOUR RIVETING ADVENTURES IN ONE FANTASTIC VOLUME!
WWW.TITANBOOKS.COM

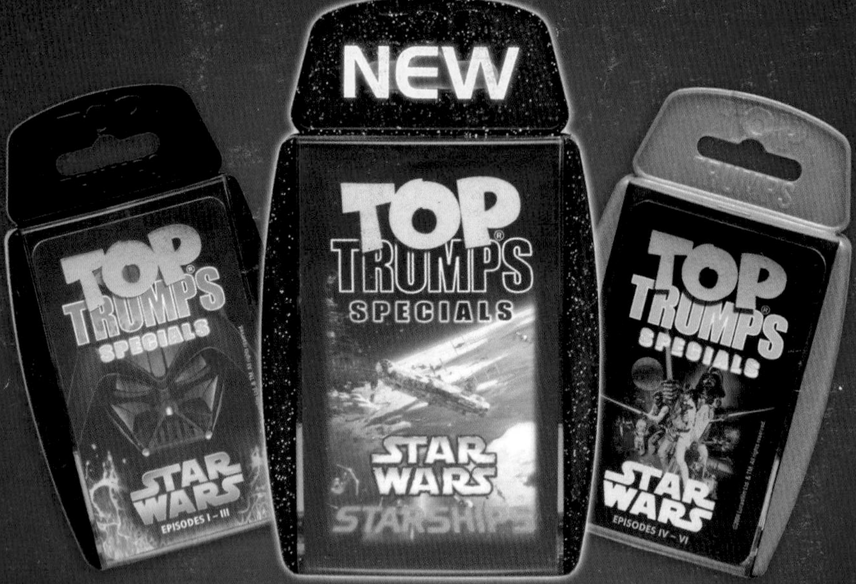
NEW
TOP TRUMPS SPECIALS
STAR WARS
EPISODES I – III
TOP TRUMPS SPECIALS
STAR WARS
STARSHIPS
TOP TRUMPS SPECIALS
STAR WARS
EPISODES IV – VI

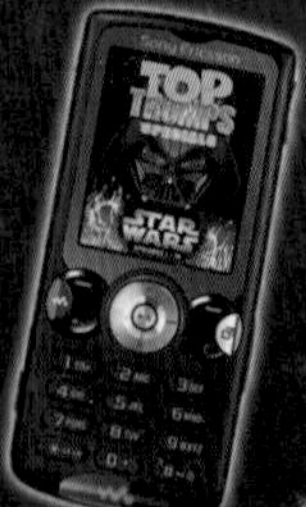
TOP TRUMPS SPECIALS
STAR WARS